swissmonographies

Casa Kalman
Luigi Snozzi

Harald R. Stühlinger

Christoph Merian Verlag

Spero che la casa le piaccia sempre, in ogni caso è quella a cui mi sento più affezionato.[1]

[1]
„Ich hoffe, dass Ihnen das Haus noch immer gefällt, für mich ist es jedenfalls dasjenige, das ich am liebsten habe." (Übersetzung HS). Luigi Snozzi an die Bauherrin, Dr. Paula Kalman. Brief vom 5.6.1979 mit der finalen Honorarrechnung. Nachlass Luigi Snozzi, Archivio del Moderno, Balerna.

"I hope that you still like the house, I regard it as my favorite." (English translation of original translation from the Italian into German: HS, translation German-English RO'D.) Luigi Snozzi to his client, Dr. Paula Kalman. Dated 5.6.1979, this letter accompanied Snozzi's final fee statement. Estate of Luigi Snozzi, Archivio del Moderno, Balerna.

Inhalt

Auftakt	14
Prolog	16
Kontext	18
Haus	30
Genese	48
Wohnstatt	70
Mythos	90
Baukultur	112
Epilog	116
Dank	124
Datenblatt	126
Quellen	127
Impressum	128

Contents

Prelude	15
Prologue	17
Context	19
House	31
Genesis	49
Abode	71
Myth	91
Building culture	113
Epilogue	117
Acknowledgements	125
Datasheet	126
Sources	127
Colophon	128

Auftakt

Dieses Buch steht am Anfang von *swissmonographies*, einer neuen Reihe von monografischen Publikationen zu ausgewählten Bauten der zweiten Hälfte des 20. Jahrhunderts in der Schweiz. Mit einem breiten Querschnitt an Beispielen – von Wohnhäusern über Geschäftsbauten bis hin zu infrastrukturellen Projekten – werden Schlaglichter auf die gebaute Umwelt des Landes geworfen. Dabei stehen Gebäude von namhaften Architektinnen und Architekten ebenso im Fokus wie solche, die weniger bekannt und rezipiert sind, aber nicht minder durch ihre hohe baukulturelle Qualität überzeugen.

 Ausgehend von einer bauhistorischen und architektonischen Beschreibung des einzelnen Bauwerks nehmen die Monografien besonders auf dessen topografische, städtebauliche und historische Rahmenbedingungen Rücksicht und ermöglichen es so, ein besseres Verständnis für den Kontext im Bauen der jeweiligen Zeit zu erlangen. Darüber hinaus werden die Rolle der Auftraggeberinnen und Auftraggeber sowie die Aneignung des Gebäudes durch die Nutzerinnen und Nutzer erläutert. Stets wird auch die Medialisierung als essenzieller Zugang für die Lesart und Deutung eines Baus und dessen Wirkung dargelegt. Dies alles soll dazu führen, die wichtigsten baukulturellen Aspekte des vorgestellten Gebäudes zu durchdringen und besser zu verstehen.

 Beabsichtigtes Ziel ist es, mit dieser Publikationsreihe Schweizer Bauwerke sowohl im In- wie im Ausland einer breiten interessierten Leserschaft bekannt zu machen und so gleichzeitig den seit dem Einsetzen des industriellen Bauens entstandenen Gebäuden eine neue Wertschätzung entgegenzubringen. Vor dem Hintergrund der ökologischen und gesellschaftlichen Herausforderungen unserer Zeit ist es unabdingbar, dass wir das bauliche Erbe aus der Zeit nach 1945 in besonderem Masse achten und uns verpflichten, es für die Zukunft zu pflegen und zu erhalten.

Prelude

This book is the first of the *swissmonographies*, a new series of monograph publications on selected buildings in Switzerland that date from the second half of the 20th century. Using a broad cross-section of examples—from residential to commercial buildings to infrastructure projects—the series showcases the built environment in this country. While focusing on buildings by famous architects, the monographs will also include works by less well-known designers, which, while perhaps not so extensively documented, are nevertheless equally convincing examples of high architectural quality.

    Starting with an architectural and historical description of the individual buildings, the monographs devote particular attention to their topographical, urban design and historical backgrounds, enabling readers to arrive at a better understanding of the context of building of the respective era. In addition, the role of the clients and the ways in which the building was appropriated by its users are described. Medialization as an essential approach to reading and interpreting a building and its impact is also addressed in each case. The intention here is to help readers grasp the most important architectural aspects of the building presented and to understand them better.

    The aim of this series of publications is to make a wide readership in Switzerland and abroad familiar with Swiss buildings and in this way to develop a new appreciation of the buildings erected since the start of industrial construction. Against the background of the ecological and social challenges presented by our times, it is essential that we devote particular attention to the legacy of buildings from the period after 1945 and commit ourselves to maintaining and preserving this legacy for the future.

Prolog

Zürichsee. Ein strahlender Samstagmorgen im September 2011. Eine betreute Ausfahrt mit einem Viererboot. Ich sitze darin, hinter mir eine Frau. Zwischen uns entspinnt sich während der Ruderübungen ein Gespräch. Fakten werden ausgetauscht. „Ich bin Psychotherapeutin." „Ich bin Assistent an der ETH am Departement Architektur." „Ah, ich interessiere mich auch für Architektur, für gute Architektur!"

Dann rudern wir los und ich frage mich während der gesamten Ausfahrt, wie für diese Frau wohl „gute Architektur" aussieht. Nach der Ausfahrt trinken wir einen Kaffee, ich erfahre ihren Namen, Vera Brunner-Kalman, der Beginn einer Freundschaft.

Brione sopra Minusio, viele Monate später. Ein erster gemeinsamer Besuch in der CK, der Casa Kalman, wie Vera ihr Ferienhaus im SMS-Verkehr abkürzt. Ich kehre öfters zu Besuchen ins Haus zurück und lerne es immer besser kennen. Über mehrere Jahre hinweg erschliesse ich mir die Räume und Winkel, geniesse die Blicke auf das Gebäude und aus den Zimmern, entdecke die Bezüge zur Umgebung, kann mich an dem Blick auf und durch die Pergola nicht sattsehen. Ich sehe, dass die Bäume Zuwendung brauchen, und beginne den Feigenbaum und den Bergahorn zu schneiden. Mein Engagement geht sogar so weit, dass ich vorschlage, einen alten und kurz nach Fertigstellung des Hauses gepflanzten Haselstrauch zu entfernen. Gemeinsam mit Simon, dem Sohn der Besitzerin, schneiden wir die Äste ab und graben den monströsen Wurzelstock mit Schaufel und Spitzhacke im Februar 2018 aus.

Wieder einmal im Tessin reift die Idee, ein Buch über das Haus herauszugeben, dem noch keine Monografie gewidmet worden ist. Der Gedanke fällt auf fruchtbaren Boden. 2021 beginnen die Arbeiten dazu.

Prologue

Lake Zurich. A bright, sunny Saturday morning in September 2011. A training session in a four-man boat. I am seated in the boat, there is a woman behind me. While the rowers are warming-up we strike up a conversation. Details are exchanged. "I'm a psychotherapist." "I am an assistant in the Department of Architecture at the ETH." "Really? I'm interested in architecture, too, I mean in good architecture!"

Then we row off and during the entire excursion I find myself asking what this woman might mean by "good architecture." After the trip we take a coffee together, I learn that her name is Vera Brunner-Kalman. It is the start of a friendship.

Brione sopra Minusio, many months later. A first joint visit to the Casa Kalman or CK, the abbreviation that Vera uses for her holiday house when writing me a text message. I make several further visits to the house, getting to know it better and better. Over a period of several years, I explore the rooms and angles, enjoy the views of the building and from the rooms, discover the relationships to the surroundings, cannot get enough of the view of and through the pergola. I see that some trees need pruning and begin to cut back the fig tree and the sycamore. My involvement goes so far that I even suggest removing an old hazelnut bush that had been planted shortly after the house was completed. Together with Simon, the owner's son, we cut off the branches and, using a spade and pickaxe, in February 2018 we dig up the enormous rootstock.

When back again in Ticino the idea of publishing a book about this house, which had never been the subject of a monograph, began to grow. The idea fell on fruitful ground and work on the book started in 2021.

Kontext

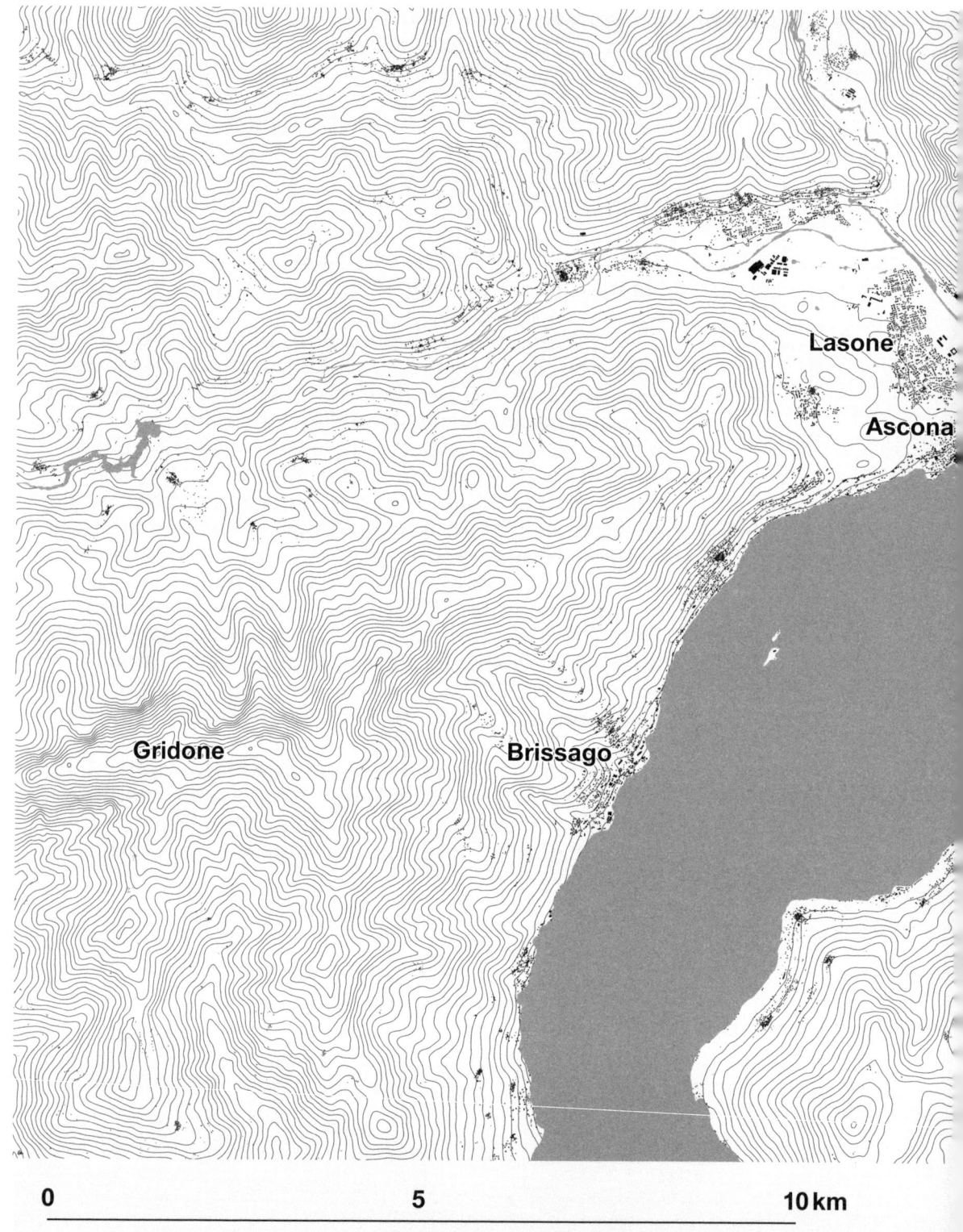

Fig. 1   Umgebungsplan, nördlicher Lago Maggiore / Surrounding map, northern Lago Maggiore

Context

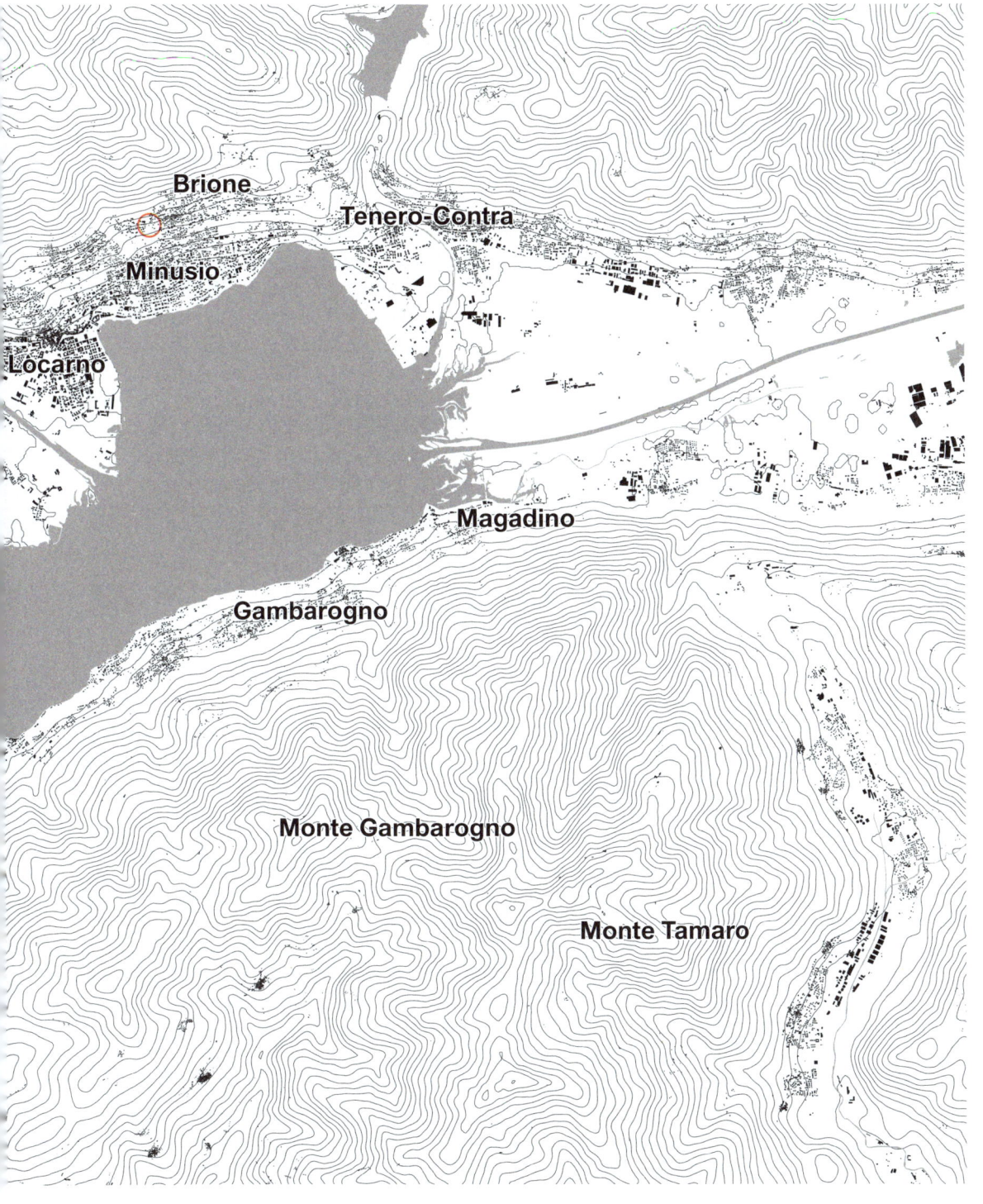

Jemand, der das erste Mal von Norden anreisend ins Tessin kommt, den Gotthard über den Pass oder durch den längsten Eisenbahntunnel der Welt quert und den nördlichsten Teil des Lago Maggiore vor Augen hat, ist überwältigt vom Zusammenspiel der Berge und des Sees, aber auch abgeschreckt von der baulichen Eroberung der Landschaft durch den Menschen. Gleich ergeht es höchstwahrscheinlich auch denen, die von Süden her ankommen. |Fig.1|

Der namensgebende Fluss des Kantons, Ticino, ergiesst sich in den Langensee – die deutsche Bezeichnung für den Lago Maggiore – und bildet bei seinem Eintritt in den See ein Delta mit verzweigten Flussläufen aus. Erst die Gewässerkorrektur zwischen 1888 und 1912 verwandelte die Magadinoebene in fruchtbares Agrarland. Die Ebene liegt knapp 200 Meter über dem Meer und wird an ihrem oberen Ende auf der Nord- und Südseite von steilen Hängen der Lepontinischen respektive der Tessiner Alpen gefasst. Der grösste Teil des Lago Maggiore befindet sich auf italienischem Staatsgebiet, erstreckt sich dort von Nord nach Süd und wird von ebenso hohen wie steilen Bergen flankiert. Locarno und Ascona liegen am Nordufer des Sees, dort, wo sich ein grosser Schwemmkegel mit dem sich beeindruckend ausdehnenden Delta der Maggia nach Südosten in den See hineinschiebt. Das historische Zentrum von Ascona liegt direkt am See, jedoch erstreckt sich die Stadt heute über den grössten Teil der südwestlichen Hälfte des Deltas. Die nördlich angesiedelte Gemeinde von Locarno hingegen teilt sich in zwei nicht zusammenhängende Gebiete: in einen Landstrich in der Magadinoebene mit dem lokalen Flughafengelände und in das davon getrennte, eigentliche Stadtgebiet auf der nordöstlichen Hälfte des Deltas. Im Gegensatz zu Ascona ist das historische Zentrum von Locarno vom Ufer des Sees abgerückt und lagert sich um die ihrem Namen gerecht werdende Piazza Grande. Diese befindet sich auf dem untersten Niveau der Stadt, die sich mit Wohnbauten hoch bis zum Stadtteil Monti Trinità den Hang hinaufzieht. |Fig.2| Im Anschluss an Locarno liegen im Osten mehrere Ortschaften mit kleinen historischen Kernen, die sich im Laufe der Zeit mit Ein- und Mehrfamilienhäusern zu einem Siedlungsteppich verwoben haben. |Fig.3| Das sind Muralto, auf dessen Ortsgebiet der Bahnhof Locarno liegt, überragt von Orselina mit der landschaftlich exponierten Pilgerkirche Madonna del Sasso, im Anschluss an Muralto die Gemeinde Minusio und das darüber befindliche Dorf Brione sopra Minusio.

Fig. 2   Ansicht von Locarno, Muralto, Minusio und Brione sopra Minusio /
View of Locarno, Muralto, Minusio and Brione sopra Minusio

Someone travelling from the north, who is visiting Ticino for the first time, crosses the Gotthard via the mountain pass or through the world's longest railway tunnel and then sees the northernmost part of Lago Maggiore, is overwhelmed by the interplay of mountains and lake, but also appalled by the buildings with which humankind has desecrated the landscape. The impression made on those coming from the south is probably much the same. |Fig.1|

The Ticino, the river that gave the canton its name, flows into Lago Maggiore and where it enters the lake it forms a delta with many branches. A regulation of the river between 1888 and 1912 transformed the Magadino Plain into fertile agricultural land. The plain is almost 200 meters above sea level and at the upper end, on both the north and south shores, it is bordered by the steep slopes of the Lepontine and Ticino Alps respectively. The larger part of Lago Maggiore is in Italy, where it extends in north-south direction and there, too, is flanked by high, steep mountains. Locarno and Ascona are on the north shore of the lake, where a large alluvial cone with the impressively expanding delta of the Maggia slides southeastwards into the lake. While Ascona's historical center lies directly on the lake, today the city extends across a major part of the southwestern half of the delta. In contrast the town of Locarno, which lies to the north, consists of two separate parts: a district on the Magadino Plain with the local airport and, separated from it on the north-eastern half of the delta,

Kontext

Fig. 3 | Siedlungsgebiet von Locarno, Muralto, Minusio und Brione sopra Minusio /
Urban fabric of Locarno, Muralto, Minusio und Brione sopra Minusio

Die Kantonsstrasse, Via Orselina respektive Via Brione, führt von der Kirche von Brione Richtung Westen nach Orselina. | Fig. 4 | **Parallel dazu verläuft die etwa 25 Meter tiefer liegende, weniger befahrene Via Panoramica, die im Westen am tief eingeschnittenen Bachlauf Riale Rabissale endet. Etwa 200 Meter westlich des Dorfzentrums von Brione führt von der Via Orselina eine schmale Strasse – ebenfalls als Via Panoramica benannt – bergab.** | Fig. 5 | **Es eröffnet sich eine Panoramaaussicht auf den sich weit nach Süden ausdehnenden Lago Maggiore, die Brissago-Inseln, das erste Städtchen auf**

the urban area. In contrast to Ascona the historic center of Locarno is set back from the lakeshore and is laid out around the appropriately named Piazza Grande. This square is at the lowest level of the city, which, with a series of residential buildings, climbs up the slope to the district of Monti Trinità. |Fig. 2| To the east of Locarno there are several towns with small historic centers, which over the course of time have formed a carpet-like settlement of single-family houses and apartment blocks. |Fig. 3| These are Muralto, where Locarno Train Station is located, above it Orselina, where the pilgrimage church of Madonna del Sasso stands at an exposed location in the landscape, next to Muralto is the municipality of Minusio and above it the village Brione sopra Minusio. The cantonal road, the Via Orselina, respectively Via Brione, leads westwards from the church in Brione to Orselina. |Fig. 4| Parallel to it, about 25 meters lower down, runs the less busy Via Panoramica, which ends in the west at the stream known as Riale Rabissale, which runs in a deep channel. Around 200 meters to west of the village center of Brione a narrow road—also called Via Panoramica—turns off Via Orselina and runs downhill. |Fig. 5| Here there is a panoramic view of Lago Maggiore

Fig. 4 — Ausblick auf den Lago Maggiore von der Via Brione oberhalb der Casa Kalman / View of Lago Maggiore from Via Brione above Casa Kalman

Fig. 5 — Ausblick von der Terrasse der Casa Kalman auf das Maggiadelta mit Locarno / View from the terrace of Casa Kalman on the Maggia delta with Locarno

Fig. 6 — Casa Kalman und der Brunnen nahe der Strassenkreuzung / Casa Kalman and the fountain near the street crossing

Fig. 7 — Blick auf die Casa Kalman, die Via Brione und den Lago Maggiore / View of Casa Kalman, Via Brione and Lago Maggiore

Kontext

italienischem Staatsgebiet, Cannobio, und die umgebenden Bergketten. Die Spitze des höchsten Gipfels, Gridone (2188 m) auf der Westseite des Sees, teilen sich die Schweiz und Italien. Wendet man sich ein wenig nach links, öffnet sich der Blick zur gegenüberliegenden Seeuferseite mit den Ortschaften Magadino und Gambarogno. Letztere ist Namensgeberin des Monte Gambarogno (1734 m), östlich davon liegt der höhere Monte Tamaro (1962 m). Schliesslich vereinigt

Fig. 8 — Typisches *Rustico* unterhalb der Casa Kalman / Typical *rustico* below the Casa Kalman

extending far to the south, of the Brissago Islands, Cannobio, the first little town on Italian territory, and of the surrounding mountain ranges. Switzerland and Italy share the summit of the highest peak, Gridone (2188 m), on the west side of the lake. If you turn slightly to the left, you have a view of the opposite shore of the lake with the towns Magadino and Gambarogno. The latter gave the name to the mountain known as Monte Gambarogno (1734 m), to the east is Monte Tamaro, which is slightly higher (1962 m). The road that runs downhill then joins the actual Via Panoramica. Water splashing in a small fountain brings the spectacular backdrop alive acoustically. |Fig. 6|

The site of the Casa Kalman lies between Via Brione and Via Panoramica. |Fig. 7| A small stream known as Riale Ramnosa flows along the eastern boundary of the site. However, it rarely carries water and at the road junction it runs beneath the Via Panoramica. Below the road, along the water course, there is a small wood with tall trees. The many chestnut trees recall the important economic role they once played for the people of Ticino. Small vineyards that are found here and there between the innumerable single-family houses indicate the wine-growing tradition, which remains a significant economic factor in Switzerland's southernmost canton. As well as the historic Ticino houses in the old village cores, there are small functional buildings, known as *rustici*, which date from the time when these areas were cultivated. |Fig. 8| Although the slopes are, in part, densely built-up, the impression everywhere is of a green landscape, which, as well as the typical Alpine trees and the chestnut trees referred to above, also has fig trees, bananas and palm trees, an indication of the special climatic conditions that prevail here. |Fig. 9| The exposed location with dramatic views of the lake and the mountains means that these slopes—much like everywhere in Ticino, whether with or without a view of the lake— offer highly desirable sites for holiday homes. Almost everywhere you can see a building crane that indicates a conversion or the erection of a new building. It is precisely the extreme steepness of the slopes that offers proof of the ingeniousness of the various building professionals, who in the case of the Casa Kalman, too, were called upon to show what they can do.

sich die hinabführende Strasse mit der eigentlichen Via Panoramica. Das Plätschern eines kleinen Brunnens belebt akustisch die spektakuläre Kulisse. |Fig. 6|

Eingespannt zwischen Via Brione und Via Panoramica befindet sich das Grundstück der Casa Kalman. |Fig. 7| Entlang der östlichen Grundstücksgrenze verläuft ein kleines Bächlein namens Riale Ramnosa, das jedoch nur selten Wasser führt und bei der Strassenkreuzung die Via Panoramica unterquert. Unterhalb der Strasse entlang des Wasserlaufs befindet sich ein Wäldchen mit mächtigen Bäumen. Die vielen Kastanienbäume legen Zeugnis von ihrer ehemaligen wirtschaftlichen Bedeutung für die Bevölkerung des Tessins ab. Kleine Weingärten, die als Relikte immer wieder zwischen den unzähligen Einfamilienhäusern auftauchen, zeugen von der Tradition des Weinbaus, der noch immer einen nicht unwichtigen Wirtschaftsfaktor des südlichsten Schweizer Kantons darstellt. Neben den historischen Tessiner Häusern in den ursprünglichen Dorfkernen finden sich kleine Nutzbauten, sogenannte *rustici*, aus der Zeit der Bewirtschaftung dieser Flächen. |Fig. 8| Obschon die Hänge zum Teil sehr dicht bebaut sind, ergibt sich allerorts ein überaus grünes Landschaftsbild, das neben den erwähnten Kastanienbäumen und typischen Alpenbäumen auch Feigenbäume, Bananenstauden und Palmen aufweist, die auf die besonderen klimatischen Verhältnisse hindeuten. |Fig. 9| Aufgrund der exponierten Lage mit dramatischen Ausblicken auf See und Berge stellen diese Hänge – wie überall im Tessin, ob mit oder ohne Seesicht – begehrte Bauplätze für Ferienhäuser dar. Kaum findet sich ein Abschnitt, in dem nicht gerade ein Baukran von einem Um- oder Neubau zeugt. Gerade der Umstand, dass es sich um sehr steile Hänge handelt, belegt die Ingeniösität der Baugewerke, welche auch bei der Errichtung der Casa Kalman einiges zu leisten hatten.

Fig. 9 — Pflanzen in nächster Umgebung des Hauses / Plants in the immediate vicinity of the house

Fig. 10 — Luftbild / Aerial view

Über drei Wege und Strassen kann man sich der Casa Kalman nähern. |Fig. 10/11| Jeder dieser Zugänge lässt das Haus auf unterschiedliche Weise aus der umliegenden Bebauung „auftauchen" und im landschaftlichen und städtebaulichen Kontext spürbar werden.

Überwindet man von Locarno über Minusio aus den teils steilen Fussweg, gelangt man an das westliche Ende der Via Panoramica. Folgt man dieser nach Osten, erkennt man bald die Pergola der Casa Kalman, wie sie hoch auf dem steilen Grundstück thront. |Fig. 12| Das Haus selbst ist anfangs noch zu erkennen, doch je näher man sich begibt, umso mehr verschwindet es hinter dem Hügel und den Bäumen. Es taucht erst wieder im Sichtfeld auf, wenn man sich an der Strassenkreuzung befindet. |Fig. 13| Nähert man sich hingegen auf der Via Panoramica von Osten her, so steht man nach der letzten Kurve plötzlich vor dem Haus. |Fig. 14| Man hat einen Standort einige Meter unterhalb des Grundstücks, sodass das Haus durch die schräge Nahansicht der Ecksituation und trotz der bescheidenen Masse monumental aufragt. Vollkommen anders verhält es sich, wenn man über den Abzweiger von der höhergelegenen Via Orselina auf das Haus zugeht. Nach einer Linkskurve

House

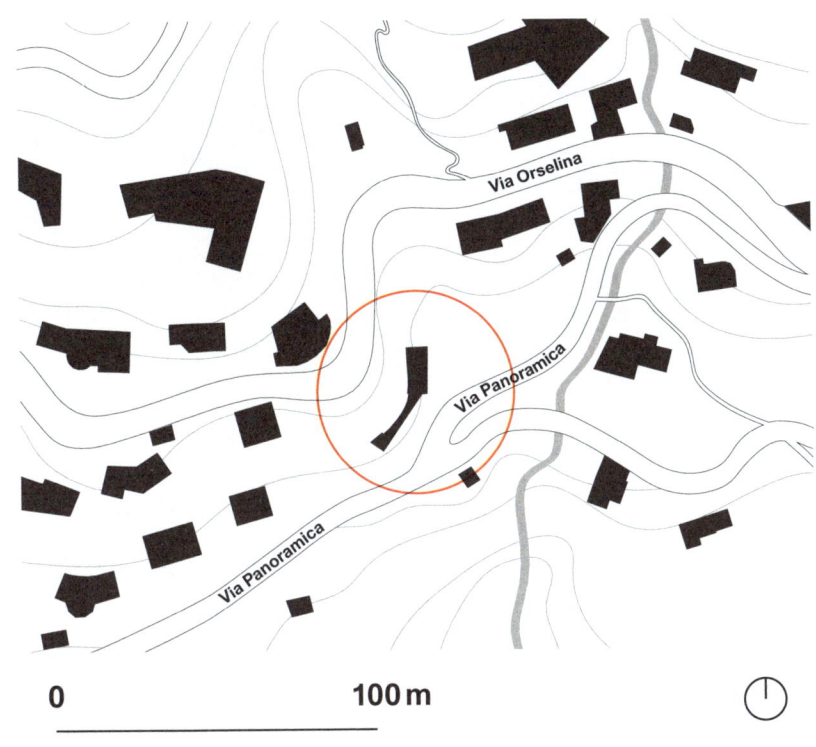

Fig. 11   Situationsplan / Site plan

You can approach the Casa Kalman via three routes and roads. |Figs.10/11| On each of these approaches the house "emerges" from the surrounding development in different ways and is registered differently in its landscape and urban design context.

If you approach on foot from Locarno via Minusio, a route that is quite steep in places, you arrive at the western end of the Via Panoramica. Continuing along this road to the west you soon see the pergola of the Casa Kalman, perched high above the steep site. |Fig.12| Initially, you can still see the house itself but, as you draw closer to it, the house seems to disappear behind the hill and the trees. |Fig.13| It only comes into sight again when you reach the road junction. In contrast, if you approach from the east, along Via Panoramica, after the last curve you suddenly find yourself standing in front of the house. |Fig.14| You are a few meters below the site so that, because you are looking at the corner from an angle, the house appears to rise monumentally in front of you, despite its modest size. When you approach the house via the road that branches off Via Orselina, which is higher up, the situation is entirely different. As you come around a left curve, the house emerges from behind a

Fig. 12
Fig. 13 — Pergola / Pergola
Schrägansicht von Südosten / Oblique view from southeast

taucht das Haus hinter einer Hecke auf und man befindet sich etwa auf Höhe des Wohngeschosses. Hier steht man frontal zur langen Ostfassade. |Fig.15| Dies ist bemerkenswert, denn kaum ein anderes Wohnhaus besitzt diese Ausrichtung, die dem Willen der Architekten, Luigi Snozzi und seinem Mitarbeiter Walter von Euw, geschuldet ist. Durch die frontale Position wirkt das Haus platt, beinahe wie eine Scheibe, und aufgrund der wenigen Öffnungen hat man den Eindruck einer gewaltigen Stützmauer im steil abfallenden Hang. Die Ostfassade ist der grösste sichtbare Teil des Hauses, denn sowohl die Nord- wie auch die Südfassade sind bedeutend schmäler und nur bedingt einsehbar, die Westfassade ragt gar nur wenige Meter aus dem Steilhang heraus und ist lediglich aus der Nähe zu sehen. Das Flachdach als fünfte Fassade des Hauses kann man von der Via Brione aus an einer Stelle zur Gänze ausmachen. |Fig. 16/17| Die Terrasse ist von der Via Panoramica nur zu erahnen, wird sie doch grösstenteils von Büschen, Sträuchern und Bäumen verdeckt. Die exponierte Pergola ist hingegen von mehreren Orten aus gut sichtbar.

hedge, and you find yourself approximately at the level of the living room floor. Here you address the long east façade frontally. |Fig.15| This is remarkable, as there is hardly any other dwelling house with this orientation nearby, which was the specific intention of architect Luigi Snozzi and his assistant Walter von Euw. Because of the frontal positioning the house seems flat, almost like a panel, and, as there are few openings, you have the impression of a powerful retaining wall in a steeply sloping site. The east façade is the largest visible part of the house, as both the north and the south façades are far narrower and are only partly visible. The west façade

Fig. 14 — Blick nach Südwesten / View towards southwest

Fig. 15 — Ostfassade / Eastern façade

Fig. 16   Blick von der Via Brione / View from Via Brione

Fig. 17 — Blick von der Via Brione / View from Via Brione

projects just a few meters out of the steep slope and can only be seen from close up. The flat roof, the fifth façade of the house, can be seen in its entirety from a point on Via Brione. |Figs. 16/17| From Via Panoramica you have just an intimation of the existence of the terrace, as it is largely concealed by bushes, shrubs, and trees. On the other hand, the exposed pergola is clearly visible from several points.

Fig. 18 Treppenaufgang zum Hauseingang / Steps to the house entrance

Fig. 19 — Blick vom Zugangsweg zum See / View from the path towards the lake

From the junction below the house, you climb twelve steps to a small, gently rising path which leads directly northwards, alongside the stream. | Fig. 18 | At the end of this path you climb a step and then turn west towards the entrance to the house. | Fig. 19 | After climbing a further five steps you reach the covered entrance area. | Fig. 20 | It is marked by a tall incision in the concrete wall in which two windows, one to the kitchen and one to a bedroom, are placed one above the other. | Fig. 21 | The entrance door is completely glazed and, like all the other doors and windows, has a green painted metal frame. Outdoors and indoors are connected by generous amounts of glazing. A powerful contrast, if you think of the solid concrete wall that you have just walked past. You recognize further contrasting elements: clear, space-shaping forms, white-painted walls, a brick-red terracotta floor, a green door. This simple color canon runs through the entire house.

The entrance level or basement story contains a storage space with laundry and a heating room with a separate tank room. From the entrance area, moving in a southerly direction, you ascend 23 steps to bring you to the living room floor. A similar staircase brings you from the living room floor to the bedroom floor above.

Fig. 20 Eingang / Entrance

Fig. 21 — Eingang / Entrance

Fig. 22 — Treppenaufgang zum Schlafgeschoss / Staircase to the bedroom floor

Fig. 23 | Balkon des Hauptschlafzimmers / Balcony of the master bedroom

Von der Kreuzung unterhalb des Hauses gelangt man über zwölf Stufen auf einen kleinen, leicht ansteigenden Weg, der entlang des Bachlaufes gerade nach Norden führt. |Fig. 18| Am Ende des Weges steigt man über eine Stufe hoch und wendet sich nach Westen zum Hauseingang. |Fig. 19| Nach weiteren fünf Stufen erreicht man den gedeckten Eingangsbereich. |Fig. 20| Der Hauseingang wird durch einen hohen Einschnitt in der Betonwand markiert, in dem zwei Fenster, eines von der Küche und das eines Schlafzimmers, übereinanderliegen. |Fig. 21| Die Haustüre ist vollkommen verglast und besitzt wie alle anderen Fenster- und Türrahmungen einen grün gestrichenen Metallrahmen. Aussen und Innen sind durch die grosszügige Verglasung miteinander verbunden. Ein grosser Kontrast, wenn man an die massive Betonwand zurückdenkt, die man gerade passiert hat. Man erkennt weitere kontrastierende Elemente: klare raumdefinierende Formen, weiss gestrichene Wände, einen ziegelroten Terrakottaboden, eine grüne Tür. Dieser einfache Farbkanon wird sich durch das ganze Haus ziehen.

Das Eingangs- respektive Kellergeschoss nimmt einen Lagerraum mit Waschküche sowie einen Heizungsraum mit separatem Tankraum auf. Vom Eingangsbereich

|Fig. 22| The main tendency of arrival in the house is inscribed in the direction of these staircases: towards the large window openings, towards the mountain panorama, towards Lago Maggiore. On both these floors the less important servant spaces are on the north side, whereas the living room and main bedroom are on the south side. While the latter is enhanced by a south-facing balcony, directly adjoining the living room there is a covered seating area followed by a long terrace. |Figs. 23–28|
As it is roughly equal in floor area to the house, this terrace almost seems over-dimensioned. On one side it describes an arc that follows the contour lines of the slope, while on the other side it is bordered by a straight retaining wall, which meets the south façade of the house at an angle of 135°. At its southwestern end it is spatially terminated by a simple but iconic pergola. The terrace is at an altitude of 416.66 meters above sea level, which is 237 meters above Lago Maggiore and, according to Luigi Snozzi, it follows the line of an old farming path.[2]

On the main floor is the kitchen, which has a small door on the north wall, the wet room with toilet and shower, the living room with an open fireplace, and,

[2] Snozzi, Luigi: Il luogo o la ricerca del silenzio / Der Ort oder die Suche nach der Stille. In: *archithese. Zeitschrift und Schriftenreihe für Architektur und Kunst.* Issue 3–84, vol. 14, Zurich 1984, p. 25.

Fig. 24 — Detail des Balkons / Detail of the balcony

Fig. 25   Ausblick vom Balkon / View from the balcony

Fig. 26   Blick unter dem Balkon bis zum Monte Tamaro /
View from beneath the balcony towards Monte Tamaro

Fig. 27 Blick vom Balkon bis zu den Brissago-Inseln /
View from the balcony towards the Brissago Islands

Fig. 28 | Blick auf Pergola und See vom Wohnzimmer aus / View from the living room towards the pergola and the lake

des Hauses gelangt man über 23 Stufen ins Wohngeschoss und strebt dabei nach Süden. Die gleiche Disposition zeigt sich im Stock darüber vom Wohn- ins Schlafgeschoss. |Fig. 22| In diesen Richtungen ist die Haupttendenz der ankommenden Bewegung innerhalb des Hauses eingeschrieben, hin zu den grössten Fensteröffnungen, hin zum Bergpanorama, hin zum Lago Maggiore. So liegen denn auf diesen zwei Geschossen im Norden die dienenden beziehungsweise untergeordneten Zimmer, im Süden hingegen das Wohnzimmer und das Hauptschlafzimmer. Während Letzteres durch einen Balkon nach Süden hin nobilitiert wird, schliessen sich an das Wohnzimmer zuerst ein gedeckter Sitzplatz und dann eine lange Terrasse an. |Fig. 23–28| Diese scheint fast überproportioniert, denn sie besitzt in etwa dieselbe Grundfläche wie das Haus. Sie zeichnet auf der einen Seite mit einem Bogen den Hang nach und auf der anderen wird sie von einer geraden Stützmauer begrenzt, die in einem Winkel von 45° an die Südfassade anschliesst. Am südwestlichen Ende erhält sie mit einer Pergola ihren einfachen, aber ikonischen räumlichen Abschluss. Die Terrasse des Hauses liegt auf 416,66 m Seehöhe, somit 237 m

to the south, the terrace. On the floor above there are two bedrooms and a second wet room area with toilet and bathtub. Although simple, this layout is spatially charged by the complex way in which the spaces interlock. Firstly, there is a two-story void between the living room and bedroom floors, |Figs. 29/30| so that from the staircase landing on the bedroom floor you can look down into the living room. |Fig. 31|

Fig. 29   Wohnzimmer mit Wintersonne / Living room with winter sun

Fig. 30 — Wohnzimmer mit offenem Kamin / Living room with the open fireplace

[2] Snozzi, Luigi: Il luogo o la ricerca del silenzio / Der Ort oder die Suche nach der Stille. In: *archithese. Zeitschrift und Schriftenreihe für Architektur und Kunst*. Heft 3–84, Jg. 14, Zürich 1984, S. 25.

über dem Lago Maggiore und zeichnet, laut Luigi Snozzi, einen alten Bauernweg nach.[2]

Im Hauptgeschoss befinden sich die Küche mit einem kleinen Austritt an der Nordwand, die Nasszelle mit Toilette und Dusche, das Wohnzimmer mit offenem Kamin sowie die Terrasse im Süden, in der Etage darüber zwei Schlafzimmer sowie die zweite Nasszelle mit Toilette und Badewanne. Diese einfache Aufteilung wird jedoch durch komplexe räumliche Verschränkungen spannungsreich aufgeladen. Zum einen gibt es einen zweigeschossigen Luftraum zwischen Wohnzimmer und Schlafgeschoss |Fig. 29/30|, sodass man auch vom Treppenabsatz im Schlafgeschoss hinunter ins Wohnzimmer blicken kann. |Fig. 31|

Fig. 31 Treppenpodest im Schlafgeschoss / Staircase landing on the bedroom floor

Genese

48

Die folgenden Pläne und Skizzen zeigen Entwurfsüberlegungen und Projektstände ab Dezember 1973 bis zu den Ausführungsplänen vom Oktober 1975.

Genesis

49

The preceding plans and sketches show design considerations and project statuses from December 1973 to the October 1975 implementation plans.

Genese

Sobald man im Architekturbüro Ende Oktober 1973 die Geometerpläne erhalten hatte, gingen Luigi Snozzi und der massgeblich an der Planung des Ferienhauses beteiligte Walter von Euw ans Werk. Das erste Vorprojekt für das aussergewöhnlich steile Grundstück lag bereits Mitte Dezember 1973 als Gesprächsgrundlage für die Besprechung mit der Auftraggeberin vor. | Fig. 32/33 |

3
Siehe S. 74.

4
Schreiben der Kommune Minusio mit den Vorgaben für die Errichtung eines Wohnhauses. Nachlass Luigi Snozzi, Archivio del Moderno, Balerna.

Ein dreigeschossiger prismatischer Bau ist so auf dem Grundstück positioniert, dass dessen Längsachse exakt in Nord-Süd-Richtung verläuft. Das Wohngeschoss wird mit einer Terrasse erweitert, die sich entlang des Hanges bis knapp an die Grundstücksgrenze im Südwesten des Bauplatzes vorschiebt. Dieses erste Projekt folgte noch den Vorgaben der Bauherrin, indem sich im Erdgeschoss, neben den Technikräumen, eine kleine Einliegerwohnung hinter einer dreijochigen Kolonnade befindet.[3] In einer Notiz von Walter von Euw an Luigi Snozzi, die diesem Projekt beigelegt wurde, weist er auf dessen Schwächen hin. Einerseits war ihm die Zugangsrampe zu steil geraten, andererseits lag die Wohnfläche bei 134 m^2 anstatt bei den bewilligten 113,40 m^2.[4] Besonderheit dieses Projektes wäre der Verlauf des Weges zum Hauseingang gewesen. Man betritt zuerst im untersten Geschoss einen gedeckten Freibereich, quert das Haus im Freien und geht dann weiter im Freien über eine Treppe zwischen Haus und Stützmauer. Sobald man auf dem Wohn- und Terrassengeschoss ankommt, kann linkerhand das Haus direkt über das Wohnzimmer betreten werden, oder man folgt dem Verlauf der Terrasse. Im Obergeschoss befinden sich zwei Schlafzimmer. Der Übergang von innen nach aussen respektive die Konzeption der Öffnungen des Gebäudes zeugt von einer verschlossenen, abweisenden Geste nach Osten bei gleichzeitiger Öffnung des Wohngeschosses nach Süden und Westen. Die Südfassade des Hauptschlafzimmers ist geschlossen, hat aber eine Fensterfront nach Westen auf einen nicht einsehbaren Bereich, der zwischen dem Hang und dem Gebäude aufgespannt ist. Die Stützmauer ist zu etwa drei Viertel mit einer Pfeilerstellung zum Hang hin geöffnet. Schon in diesem ersten Entwurf wird die besonders konzipierte Verschränkung von Innenraum, überdachter, im Freien befindlicher Transitionszone und Terrasse sichtbar. Die zweiläufige Erschliessungstreppe wird ebenso wie der Eingang in Querrichtung am Nordende des Hauses platziert und erhält ein spitz ausgestülptes Treppenhaus als Erker, welcher das Volumen des Prismas aufbricht.

Genesis

As soon as the surveyor's plans arrived in the architect's office at the end of October 1973, Luigi Snozzi set to work together with Walter von Euw, who played a significant role in the design of the holiday house. By mid-December 1973 they had produced an initial project for the exceptionally steep site which provided a basis for discussions with the client. |Figs. 32/33|

[3] See pp. 73–74.

[4] Letter from the municipality of Minusio listing the regulations regarding the erection of a dwelling house. Estate of Luigi Snozzi, Archivio del Moderno, Balerna.

A three-story prismatic building is positioned on the site in such a way that its long axis runs precisely in a north-south direction. The living room floor is extended by a terrace that runs across the slope, extending almost as far as the plot boundary in the southwest of the site. This first project still followed the client's specifications, in as far as the ground floor, in addition to the rooms for the services, also has a small granny flat behind a three-bay colonnade.[3] In a note attached to this project, which Walter von Euw sent to Luigi Snozzi, von Euw points out several weaknesses. On the one hand he found the approach ramp too steep, on the other the residential floor area amounted to 134 m^2 instead of the approved figure of 113.40 m^2.[4] A special feature of this project is the path leading to the entrance. On the lowest level you first enter a covered outdoor area and then, still outdoors, you climb a flight of steps positioned between the house and the retaining wall. Having arrived on the level of the living room and terrace, you can enter the house directly through the living room on the left or you can continue along the terrace. On the upper floor there are two bedrooms. The transition from inside to outside and the concept of the openings in the building make a closed, uninviting gesture in an easterly direction, whereas the living room floor opens towards the south and the west. While the south façade of the main bedroom is closed, it has a window front facing west, towards a part of the site between the slope and the building that cannot be seen into. Around three-quarters of the retaining wall opens towards the slope through a row of columns. In this first design the specially conceived way in which indoor space, the covered outdoor transitional zone, and the terrace interlock is already evident. The two-flight staircase, like the entrance, is placed crossways at the northern end of the house, while a pointed staircase hall projecting out of the building forms a bay that interrupts the volume of the prism.

In February 1974 Snozzi's office worked on a second three-story version. The approach route first runs northwards, then it makes a turn and arrives at the entrance at the middle of the east façade. The aim

Genese

[5] Notiz Walter von Euw an Luigi Snozzi vom 17.12.1973. Nachlass Luigi Snozzi, Archivio del Moderno, Balerna.

Im Februar 1974 arbeitete man im Büro Snozzi an einer zweiten dreigeschossigen Variante. Der Zugangsweg führt zuerst nach Norden, kehrt und erreicht dann den mittig in der Ostfassade liegenden Eingang. Damit sollte der Weg verlängert werden, denn im Erstentwurf war er noch zu steil geraten.[5] Die einläufigen Treppen liegen an der Ostfassade und steigen, anders als im Erstentwurf, nun in Richtung Norden an. Während im älteren Entwurf Terrasse und Haus baulich miteinander verschränkt werden, sind Haus und Terrasse nun als separate Elemente behandelt. In diesem Entwurf folgt, anders als im Erstentwurf, auch das Nordende der Stützmauer dem Hangverlauf. Das Haus selbst behält aber seine strenge prismatische Form.

Ende März 1974 lag ein neuer, weiterentwickelter Entwurf vor. | Fig. 34/35 | Das unterste Geschoss des mittlerweile auf vier Geschosse erweiterten Baus betritt man auf Strassenniveau über einen separaten Eingang von Osten her. Hier sind Haustechnik und Keller untergebracht. Im höherliegenden Geschoss befinden sich wieder eine kleine Wohneinheit und eine Waschküche sowie darüber ein Wohn- sowie ein Schlafgeschoss. Anders sind hier der Zugang und die Treppenführung geregelt: Nach dem Betreten des Hauses führt eine einläufige Treppe entlang der Hangmauer nach Süden auf das Wohngeschoss, darüber jene auf das Schlafgeschoss zu. Diese Disposition sollte in der Folge bis zum endgültigen Projekt perpetuiert werden. Die Ostfassade ist bis auf den vertikalen Einschnitt beim Hauseingang vollkommen geschlossen. Das Wohnzimmer weist nach Westen eine vollständige Verglasung und nach Süden ein Fenster auf. Dem Hauptschlafzimmer ist eine Art Loggia, mit Öffnungen nach Süden und Westen, zugeschlagen. Die Stützmauer, die gleichzeitig zur Westfassade wird, hat inzwischen nur mehr eine, aber noch immer sehr grosse Öffnung. Mit diesem Projekt wurde schliesslich der erste Bauantrag an die Kommune gestellt. Per 11. Juni 1974 erhielt das Gesuch jedoch eine Absage, denn der Zonenplan limitierte auf diesem Grundstück die Bauhöhe auf 7,80 m mit maximal drei Geschossen.

Diesen Rückschlag nahm man aufseiten der Planer gelassen hin und parierte kurzerhand mit einem dreigeschossigen Entwurf wenige Zeit später. | Fig. 36/37 | Die ursprünglichen Grundrisse von Wohn- und Schlafgeschoss bleiben unverändert, die Einliegerwohnung wird fallengelassen und die Technikräume und die

[5] Note from Walter von Euw to Luigi Snozzi, dated 17.12.1973. Estate of Luigi Snozzi, Archivio del Moderno, Balerna.

here was to make the route longer, as in the first design it had been too steep.[5] The straight staircases are on the east façade and unlike in the first design, they rise in a northward direction. While in the earlier design the terrace and house are connected with each other, here house and terrace are treated as separate elements. In this design, unlike in the earlier proposal, the northern end of the retaining wall also follows the contour of the slope. However, the house itself retains its strictly prismatic form.

A new design produced at the end of March 1974 represented a further development. |Figs. 34/35| The height of the building was increased to four stories, the lowest floor is now entered at road level from the east through a separate entrance. The building services and cellar are on this level. On the floor above there is a small dwelling unit and a laundry, above that is the living room floor and above it the bedroom floor. In this design the approach and staircase are handled differently: when you enter the house a straight staircase runs southwards along the wall up to the living room floor, above it there is a second staircase leading up to the bedroom floor. This layout was retained and formed part of the final project. The east façade is completely closed, apart from a vertical slit at the entrance to the house. The living room is entirely glazed on the west side and has a south-facing window. The main bedroom has a kind of loggia with openings facing south and west. The retaining wall, which is also the west façade, now has just one, albeit very large, opening. This project formed the basis for the first planning application submitted to the local authority. On June 11, 1974, planning permission was refused, as the zoning plan for this site restricted the building height to 7.80 meters and a maximum of three stories.

Unfazed by this set-back, the planners respond a short time later with a three-story design. |Figs. 36/37| The plans of the living room and bedroom floors remain unaltered. The granny flat is omitted and the services rooms and the laundry on the lower level of the building are combined. The north and south façades from the earlier design are adopted unchanged. On the east façade eight small, upright rectangular windows that provide light for the basement make their first appearance. Up to this fourth project the terraces always have just a retaining wall on the uphill side and end in a flight of steps leading up to the site. This project was

Waschküche führt man im Untergeschoss zusammen. Auch Nord- und Südfassade werden unverändert übernommen, an der Ostfassade tauchen erstmals acht kleine, hochrechteckige Fenster zur Belichtung des Kellergeschosses auf. Bis zu diesem vierten Projektstand besitzen die Terrassen lediglich eine Stützmauer auf der Hangseite und enden mit einem Treppenaufgang auf das Grundstück. Dieses Projekt wurde am 3. Juli 1974 eingereicht sowie einige Tage später an die Bauherrinnen nach Zürich gesandt. Im Sommer durchlief das Projekt die fachliche Prüfung, und während man auf den Bescheid wartete, zeichnete man im Büro Fassadenentwürfe unter Verwendung verschiedener Materialien wie Back- oder Naturstein. Zwischenzeitlich wurden im August 1974 die Baugespanne auf dem Grundstück aufgestellt und das Bauvorhaben angezeigt. Das Baugesuch erhielt schliesslich am 21. November 1974 seine offizielle Genehmigung.

Im Nachlass des Büros haben sich aus den ersten drei Monaten des Jahres 1975 umfangreiche Planunterlagen erhalten, die die intensive Arbeit am und die Konkretisierung des Projektes belegen. Unzählige Skizzen vermitteln den intensiven Aushandlungsprozess für die Formfindung des Hauses. | Fig. 38, 47–50 |

Während die Planstände von Januar und Februar 1975 einige grundsätzliche formale und architektonische Ideen aus den älteren Projekten übernehmen, tauchen wesentliche Neuerungen auf. | Fig. 39/40 | Das Wohngeschoss wird im Verhältnis zum Schlafgeschoss zurückversetzt und das obere Geschoss auf zwei Betonstützen gestellt. Die Terrasse erhält einen architektonischen Abschluss in Form einer Pergola, die in Längsrichtung auf beiden Seiten mit Wänden begrenzt ist. Weitere neue Entwurfsentscheidungen werden in dieser heissen Phase des Projekts von Januar bis März 1975, für die die meisten Pläne vorliegen, getroffen. | Fig. 41/42 | Der frühere Zwickelraum zwischen Stützmauer und Westfassade wird in das Wohnzimmer inkorporiert. Dadurch ändert sich die formale Konzeption des Hauses sowie der Bezug von Innen- zu Aussenraum massgeblich. In der Westfassade befindet sich noch immer eine grosse Öffnung, die nun konsequenterweise mit einem Fenster geschlossen ist. Die Ostfassade zeigt wieder die hochrechteckigen Fenster des Kellergeschosses und neu das niedrige Bandfenster im Wohngeschoss. Die Südfassade wurde noch mehr geöffnet und die Blickachse aus dem Wohnzimmer nun

Fig. 47 | Skizzenblatt mit Perspektivenstudien, undatiert / Sketch sheet with perspective studies, undated

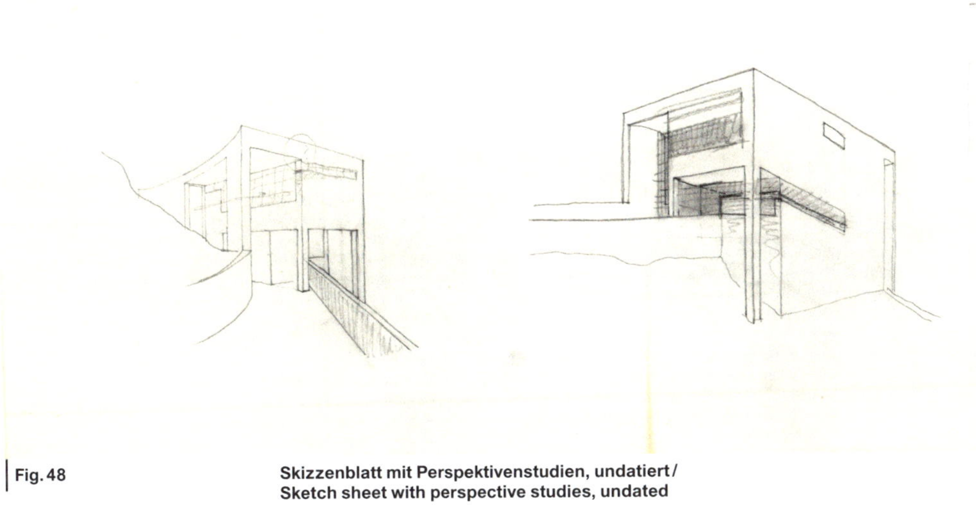

Fig. 48 | Skizzenblatt mit Perspektivenstudien, undatiert / Sketch sheet with perspective studies, undated

submitted on July 3, 1974, and a few days later was sent to the client in Zurich. | Figs. 36/37 | In summer, the project was examined by the authorities and, while the decision was awaited, various façade designs using a variety of materials such as brick or stone were drawn in the office. In August 1974, a mock-up was erected on the site to give an idea of the building project. The application was finally officially approved on November 21, 1974.

Genese

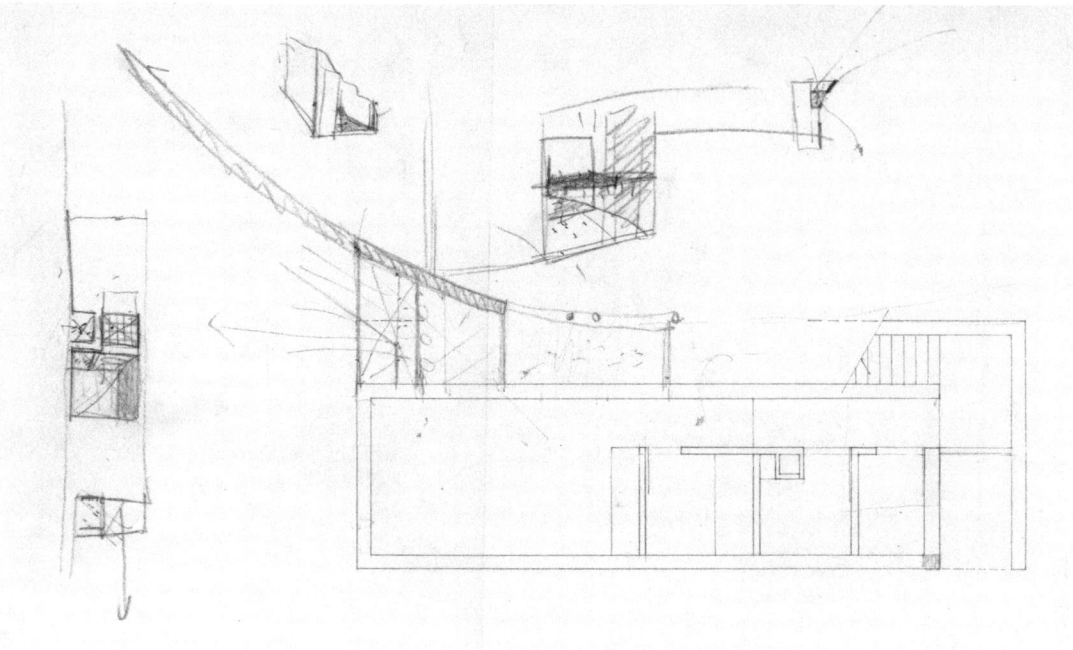

Fig. 49 Skizzenblatt mit Grundriss- und Perspektivenstudien, undatiert /
Sketch sheet with floor plans and perspective studies, undated

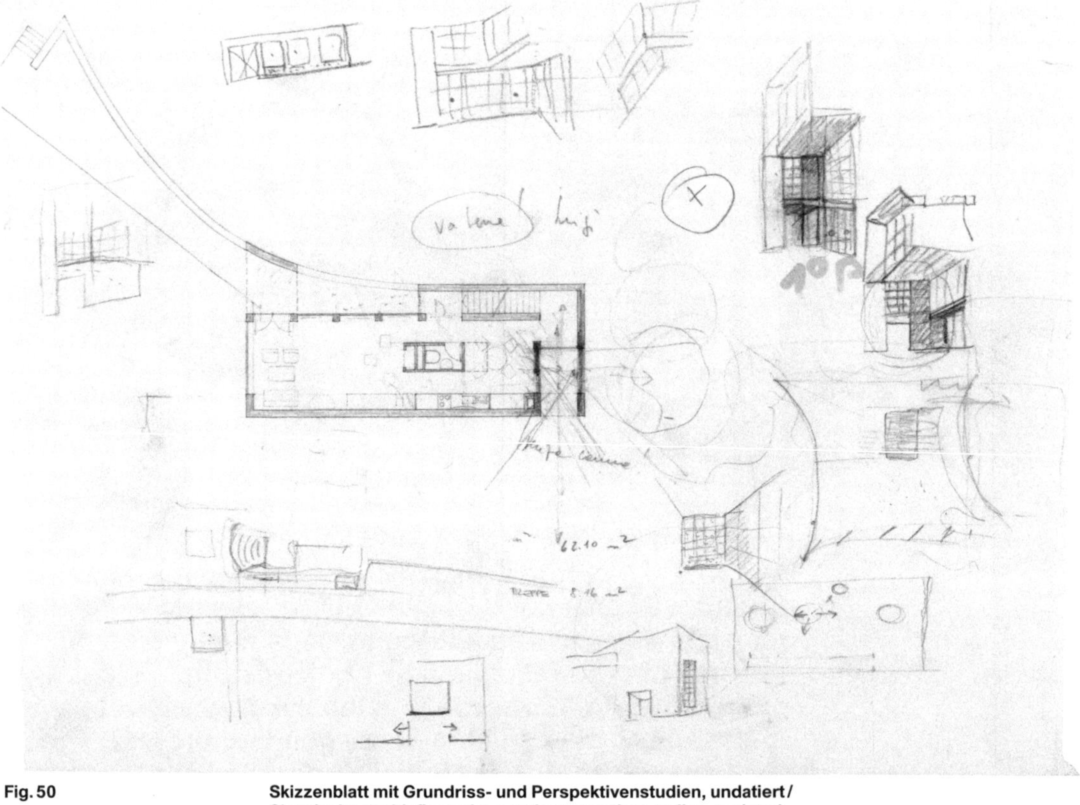

Fig. 50 Skizzenblatt mit Grundriss- und Perspektivenstudien, undatiert /
Sketch sheet with floor plans and perspective studies, undated

Numerous plan documents from the first three months of 1975 that have survived among the papers from Snozzi's office illustrate the concentrated work on the project and show how the building took concrete shape. Innumerable sketches convey the intensive negotiation process that led to the form of the house. |Figs. 38, 47–50|

While the plans from January and February 1975 include several formal and architectural ideas from the earlier projects, they also have several important new features. |Figs. 41/42| The living room floor is set back in relation to the bedroom floor, with the upper floor carried on two concrete columns. The terrace is terminated in an architectural fashion by a pergola, which is defined on both long sides by walls. In this highly important phase of the project, which extended from January to March 1975, further new design decisions were made and most of the plans date from this time. The angular space between the retaining wall and the west façade in the earlier versions is now incorporated in the living room. This had a major impact on the formal concept of the house and on the relationship between indoor and outdoor space. The large opening in the west façade is retained but now a window is placed in it. The east façade still has the upright windows to the basement as well as a new low ribbon window to the living room floor. The south façade is opened up more, and the view from the living room is now directed towards the pergola. A steel staircase leads from the living room floor to the bedroom floor above. From the upper landing you can enter the two bedrooms and the bathroom, or you can walk through a door, westwards, onto the site. In this phase of the planning the main bedroom was lit only from the south and was still separated by a wall from the void to the living room floor. While the concept for the living room and bedroom floors had, essentially, been agreed upon quite some time earlier, the meticulous planning work now focused on creating a harmonious layout for the basement.

As the planning work progressed, the understanding of the site grew deeper and clearer. It was only at a later point that the two architects realized that the topography made an opening in the west façade impossible. This deeper understanding is also reflected by the different zero levels. In December 1973, the zero level is given incorrectly as 400 meters. Throughout 1974 until April 1975 a zero level of 414,50 meters was used, after that it was fixed at 414 meters. This had

[6] Intervista a Architetto Luigi Snozzi (s.d.). https://www.youtube.com/watch?v=YSJ37FCZ9Hs (abgerufen am 18.2.2022).

mehr in Richtung Pergola gelenkt. Das Schlafgeschoss erreicht man vom Wohngeschoss über eine eingehängte Stahltreppe. Vom oberen Podest gelangt man in die beiden Schlafzimmer und das Bad oder über eine Tür westwärts auf das Grundstück. In diesem Planstand ist das Hauptschlafzimmer nur von Süden belichtet und noch durch eine Wand vom Luftraum aus dem Wohngeschoss getrennt. Während die Konzeptionen von Wohn- und Schlafgeschoss bereits seit Längerem prinzipiell feststanden, arbeitete man akribisch an einer stimmigen Disposition für das Kellergeschoss.

Im Laufe der Planungen zeigte sich das immer bessere Verständnis des Geländes. So wurde den beiden Architekten erst zu einem späten Zeitpunkt klar, dass aufgrund der Topografie eine Öffnung in der Westfassade unmöglich war. Darüber hinaus bildet sich dieses bessere Verständnis anhand der unterschiedlichen Nullpunkte ab. Im Dezember 1973 wird dieser fälschlicherweise mit 400 m angegeben. Das Jahr 1974 über hindurch bis April 1975 wurde dann mit einer Referenz von 414,50 m gearbeitet, woraufhin man sich schliesslich ab 24. April 1975 auf einen Nullpunkt von 414 m bezog. Dies hing unter anderem mit den Bebauungsbestimmungen für das Grundstück zusammen. Laut Aussage von Luigi Snozzi musste man vor der Bauabnahme beim südöstlichen Eckpunkt des Hauses noch Erde aufschütten, damit die erlaubte Gesamthöhe nicht überschritten wurde.[6]

Nach einer längeren Pause erarbeitete man im Juli 1975 den – beinahe – endgültigen Plan. |Fig. 43| Der Grundriss des Hauses zeigt noch immer an zwei Enden die gebogene Hangmauer. Das Keller- und das Wohngeschoss weisen bereits die später ausgeführten Grundrisse auf. Lediglich das Schlafgeschoss zeigt den Zwischenstand vom Februar des Jahres, denn es gibt noch eine raumhohe Trennwand zwischen Zimmer und Luftraum. Auch ist die Treppe zum Schlafgeschoss noch immer als eingehängte Stahltreppe ausgewiesen. Die Westfassade ist nun zur Gänze geschlossen, denn die überaus steile Hangsituation lässt keine sichere, grossflächige Öffnung zu. Bei der Ausdehnung der Terrasse war man sich noch unschlüssig, wie die Skizzen auf dem Gesamtplan zeigen.

Die erhaltenen Ausführungspläne datieren zwar erst auf Oktober 1975, doch bereits in früheren Plänen wurden die markantesten Änderungen, wie sie im Ausführungsplan aufscheinen, skizziert. |Fig. 44–46|

Genesis

6 Intervista a Architetto Luigi Snozzi (s.d.). https://www.youtube.com/watch?v=YSJ37FCZ9Hs (retrieved on 18.2.2022).

7 Plans of the "Facciata est" from 24.1.1975 and 27.2.1975. Estate of Luigi Snozzi, Archivio del Moderno, Balerna.

to do in part with the planning regulations that applied to the site. Luigi Snozzi once said that earth had to be piled up at the south-east corner of the house before the building inspection so that it did not exceed the permitted total height.[6]

After a longer break, what was—almost—the final plan was produced in July 1975. |Fig. 43| The floor plan of the house still shows the retaining wall with a curve at either end. The plans of the basement and the living room floor show what was later built. Only the bedroom floor reflects the intermediate stage from February of the same year, as there is still a full-height partition wall between the room and the void. The stairs leading to the bedroom floor is still shown as a steel construction hung between the two stories. The west façade is now closed completely, as the extremely steep slope made a large opening in this wall impossible. The sketches on the plan indicate that a firm decision about the extent of the terrace had not yet been reached.

Although the surviving detail plans are dated October 1975, the most striking changes found in these detail plans had already been sketched on the earlier plans. |Figs. 44–46| In the final design the retaining wall, which forms the external wall of the house at the northern end, and the terrace—which was itself extended—were straightened. The partition in the main bedroom was reduced to a parapet wall, and the staircase from the living room floor to the bedroom floor above was now made of in situ concrete. In addition, the parapet to the ribbon window on the living room floor was reduced in height so that the window now had a clear height of 98 cm rather than the previous 40 cm.[7] This has been confirmed by Vera Brunner-Kalman, who remembers that Snozzi only made this decision at a late stage, which led to him having this concrete wall, which had already been built, reduced in height. This was done to provide a better view from the living room of the mountain panorama to the east. At this stage of the project the window was still divided up into very small squares (each about 20 × 20 cm), but in the final plan from February 1976 it is made up of larger sections (around 70 × 70 cm).

The final plans for the terrace date from December 12, 1975, when construction of the house was already far advanced. Like all the routes, both inside the house and outdoors, it serves as a kind of walking aid for this steep site with a 100 percent slope and makes crossing it easier and safer.

[7] Planstände der „Facciata est" vom 24.1.1975 und 27.2.1975. Nachlass Luigi Snozzi, Archivio del Moderno, Balerna.

[8] Brief vom 18.5.1988 vom Architekturbüro an Paula Kalman. Nachlass Luigi Snozzi, Archivio del Moderno, Balerna.

Im Letztstand wurde die Stütz- respektive Aussenmauer des Hauses am nördlichen Ende wie auch die Terrasse – bei gleichzeitiger Verlängerung derselben – begradigt. Die Trennwand im Hauptschlafzimmer wurde auf eine Brüstungswand abgesenkt und die Treppe vom Wohn- zum Schlafgeschoss in Ortbeton konzipiert. Darüber hinaus ist das Parapet für das Bandfenster im Wohngeschoss an der Ostfassade abgesenkt, sodass es nunmehr eine lichte Höhe von 98 anstatt den vormaligen 40 cm hat.[7] Dies bestätigt Vera Brunner-Kalman, die sich an diese späte Entscheidung Snozzis erinnert, die dazu führte, dass er die bereits fertig betonierte Wand absenken liess. Grund dafür war, dass man dadurch das Bergpanorama im Osten besser vom Wohnzimmer aus geniessen konnte. Die bis zu diesem Projektstand sehr kleinformatige (etwa 20 × 20 cm) Fensterteilung wurde in der Ausführungsplanung im Februar 1976 zugunsten einer grösseren (etwa 70 × 70 cm) aufgegeben.

Die endgültigen Pläne zur Terrasse datieren auf den 12. Dezember 1975, als das Haus bereits weit fortgeschritten war. Sie dient, wie alle Wege im Inneren und im Freien, als eine Art Gehhilfe für das steile Grundstück mit 100 Prozent Hangsteigung, das dadurch einfach und sicher zu begehen ist.

Im Juni oder spätestens im Juli 1975 begann man mit dem Aushub der Baugrube. | Fig. 51/52 | Als das Haus, das nur eine Senkgrube hatte, 1988 an die kommunale Kanalisation angeschlossen wurde, kam es zu einem nicht unwesentlichen Eingriff in die Bausubstanz. Das niedrige, auf der Ostseite des Hauses angegliederte Volumen für die Abwasserinfrastruktur wurde im April 1988 entfernt, da diese obsolet geworden war. Das führte dazu, dass seither das Haus auf der gesamten Ostfassade aus dem Boden emporsteigt. Im Zuge dieser Umbauarbeiten wurde ein vom Architekturbüro beauftragtes Geländer für die Eingangstreppe angebracht.[8]

Ein Element, das stets bei der Betrachtung älterer Fotografien der Casa Kalman ins Auge sticht, ist die grosse Antenne auf dem Flachdach. Diese erfüllte niemals ihren Zweck, denn das Haus wurde zu keinem Zeitpunkt mit einem Fernseher ausgestattet. Wann diese schliesslich abgebaut wurde, ist nicht mehr eruierbar, jedoch stand sie noch bis nach der Jahrtausendwende. | Fig. 53 |

Fig. 51   Drei Baustellenfotos, „ca. 25.7.1975" / Three photographs of the construction site, "ca. 25.7.1975"

Genese

Casa Kalmann Minusio

settembre /ottobre 1975

piano cantina
a- riempimento con sassi
   sul posto dalle fonda-
   zioni al piano cantina
b- disarmo parete dal
   piano cantina al i.p.

sostegno lato est(riale)

| Fig. 52 | Drei Baustellenfotos, September/Oktober 1975/
Three photographs of the construction site, September/October 1975 |

[8] Letter dated 18.5.1988 from the architect's office to Paula Kalman. Estate of Luigi Snozzi, Archivio del Moderno, Balerna.

Work on excavating the site started in June or, at the latest, July 1975. | Figs. 51/52 | When the house, which originally only had a septic tank, was connected to the local drainage system in 1988 a serious intervention was made in the building fabric. In April 1988, a low building attached to the east side of the house that housed the wastewater infrastructure was removed, as it had become obsolete. Since then, the entire east façade of the house has risen directly out of the ground. In the course of this construction work the entrance steps were given a railing, which the architect's office was commissioned to design.[8]

On looking at older photographs of Casa Kalman one element that always stands out is the big antenna on the flat roof. This never served its intended purpose, as the house never had a TV. It is no longer possible to discover when it was finally removed, but it was certainly still standing there after the start of the new millennium. | Fig. 53 |

CASA DR. KALMAN BRIONE s/MINUSIO ESTERNO

Fig. 53 Alberto Flammer, vier Fotografien kurz nach Baufertigstellung, undatiert /
Alberto Flammer, four photographs shortly after completion of construction, undated

Dreissig Jahre nach der Errichtung der Casa Kalman nahm Vera Brunner-Kalman Kontakt mit Luigi Snozzi auf. Sie hatte, gemeinsam mit ihren beiden Kindern, das südlich anschliessende, noch nicht bebaute Grundstück per 28. Juni 1996 erworben. Um eine rentable Lösung für die zu tätigenden Investitionen zu finden, wurde der Architekt beauftragt, eine Studie für die Überbauung der Nachbarparzelle zu erarbeiten. |Fig. 54/55|
Wenn auch der zweite Bau als paralleles Gegenstück zur älteren Casa Kalman am Plan zu lesen ist, präsentiert sich hier eine andere Setzung: Nicht dem Hang folgend wird das Haus positioniert, sondern ähnlich einem Terrassenhaus quer in den Hang geschoben. Die Grundrissfläche ist exakt gleich lang wie jene der Casa Kalman, jedoch ein wenig breiter. Die Garage als unterstes Element wird teilweise in den Hang gebaut wie das viergeschossige Wohnhaus. Der Körper des neuen Hauses wird so weit den Hang hinaufgeschoben, dass die Aussicht der Casa Kalman nicht beeinträchtigt wird. Durch diese Lage orientiert sich das Haus zur gegenüberliegenden Seeuferseite. Das Thema des Zuganges zum Haus wird von der Garage aus kunstvoll inszeniert. Über eine einläufige Treppe gelangt man auf das Dach des Autounterstellplatzes und vollzieht eine 270-Grad-Drehung, bei der man den Blick über den ganzen See schweifen lässt. Über eine weitere einläufige Treppe gelangt man zum überdachten Eingangsbereich des Hauses. Die östliche Wand weitet sich am südlichen Ende, was man als – modische – Reminiszenz auf die Casa Kalman lesen kann. Ost- und Westwand weisen jeweils Öffnungen auf, die in frühen Projektständen auch bei der Casa Kalman vorgesehen waren. Es scheint fast so, dass Snozzi in den Entwurf einige unrealisierte Projektideen aus der Casa Kalman hier zur Umsetzung bringen wollte, die er schon Jahre zuvor in der Casa Bianchetti (1975–1977) oder in der Casa Heschl (1983–1984) in Agarone realisieren konnte. Zur Umsetzung dieser Projektentwicklung am Nebengrundstück kam es jedoch nicht, auch weil Luigi Snozzi mit dem Projekt nicht zufrieden war.

Thirty years after the completion of the Casa Kalman, Vera Brunner-Kalman contacted Luigi Snozzi. On June 28, 1996, together with her two children, she had acquired the still undeveloped site that bordered Casa Kalman directly to the south. To find a financially viable solution for the investments needed, the architect was commissioned to prepare a study for the development of the neighboring plot. |Figs. 54/55| Although the second building can be read as a parallel counterpart to the older Casa Kalman, it is positioned differently. Rather than running across the slope, the house is slid into it, like a stepped building. In plan it is exactly as long as the Casa Kalman, but somewhat wider. The garage, the lowest element, is built partly into the slope, as is the four-story house. The volume of the new building is slid far enough up the slope to prevent it blocking the view from the Casa Kalman. The house is positioned so that it faces towards the opposite shore of the lake. The theme of the approach to the house is artfully presented, starting from the garage. A staircase leads up to the carport roof, where you make a 270 degree turn that allows your gaze to roam across the entire lake. A further staircase leads to the covered entrance area to the house. The eastern wall widens at the southern end, which can be read as a direct reference to the Casa Kalman. The east and west wall have openings that are to be found in the earlier versions of the Casa Kalman project, too. It almost seems as if in this design Snozzi wanted to implement several unrealized ideas from the Casa Kalman, which he had been able to use years earlier in the Casa Bianchetti (1975–1977), or in the Casa Heschl (1983–1984) in Agarone. However, the project for the plot beside the Casa Kalman never came to fruition, among other things because Luigi Snozzi was not satisfied with it.

Genese

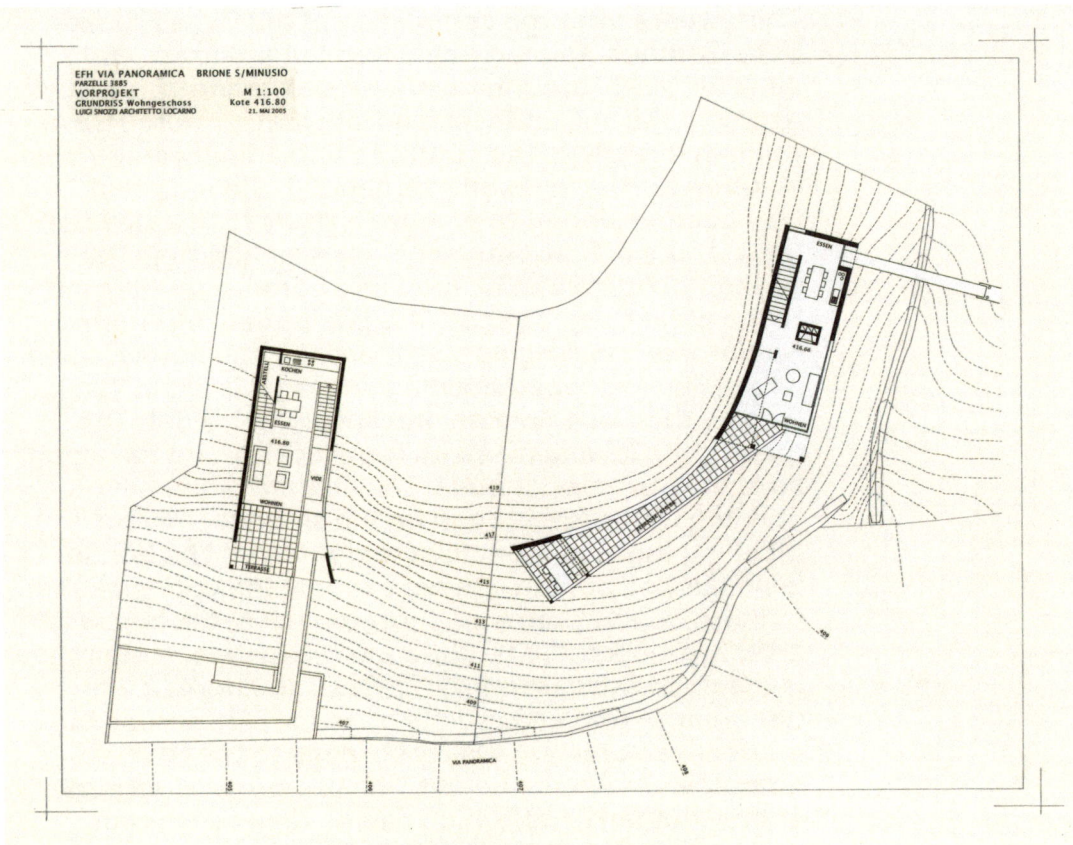

Fig. 54 Ansichten und Schnitte des Zubaus, 21. Mai 2005 /
Elevations and sections of the extension, May 21, 2005

Genesis

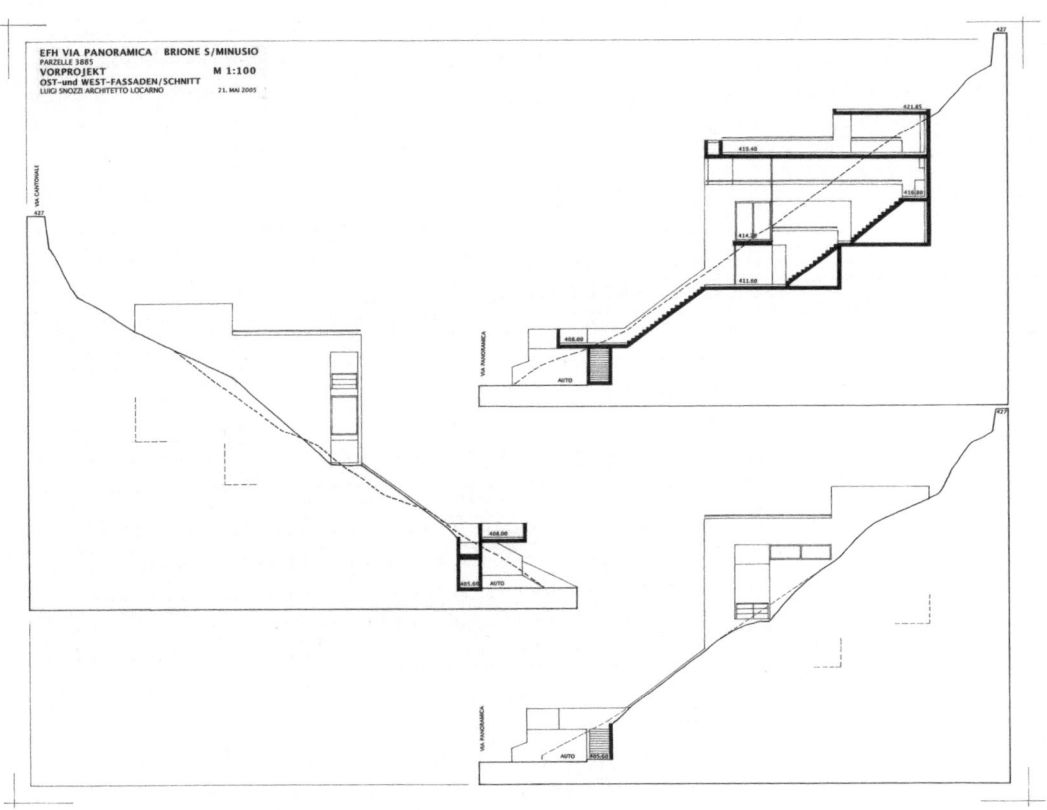

Fig. 55　　Grundriss Wohngeschoss des Zubaus, 21. Mai 2005 /
　　　　　Floor plan living room floor of the extension, May 21, 2005

Die Casa Kalman hatte eigentlich zwei Bauherrinnen: Paula Kalman-Fränkel (1915–2016), Kinderärztin in Zürich-Schwamendingen, und ihre Tochter, Vera Brunner-Kalman, Juristin und Psychotherapeutin. Im September 2021 stand Letztere (VB) dem Autor (HS) Rede und Antwort in einem Gespräch über die Casa Kalman.[9]

[9] Gespräch in der Casa Kalman am 18.9.2021.

HS Warum wollte deine Mutter ins Tessin?
VB Meine Grosseltern mütterlicherseits kamen aus Krakau. Auf ihrer Hochzeitsreise in die Schweiz, 1914, mussten sie wegen des Ausbruchs des Ersten Weltkrieges hierbleiben. Mein Grossvater, Dr. Leon Fränkel, hat daraufhin, obwohl er in Krakau als Anwalt gearbeitet hatte, seinen Lebensunterhalt durch die Herstellung und den Verkauf von Feinlederwaren bestritten. Er war immer stolz darauf, dass er während der Krisenzeiten der 1930er- und 1940er-Jahre nie einen Arbeiter entlassen musste und auch darauf, dass er immer sozialistisch gewählt hatte. Er bedauerte zeitlebens, dass er keine Immobilie besessen hatte. Während er selbst noch seiner Unternehmenstätigkeit nachging, führte er die Buchhaltung für meine Mutter, die als Kinderärztin arbeitete und die Bürden einer Alleinerzieherin zu tragen hatte. Damit wusste er stets über ihre finanzielle Situation Bescheid.

Da meine Grossmutter früh gestorben war, kümmerte sich meine Mutter um meinen Grossvater und verbrachte jedes Jahr die Ferien mit ihm im Haus von Freunden in Brione sopra Minusio. Ihr Haus war einfach und lag hervorragend, meine Mutter war davon beeindruckt. Von daher rührte die Idee eines Ferienhauses im Tessin. Es war vor allem mein Grossvater, der meine Mutter drängte, ein Ferienhaus zu kaufen. Zuerst überlegten wir, wo es sich befinden könnte, und haben dann angefangen Häuser, die zum Verkauf standen, zu suchen. Für meine praktisch veranlagte Mutter war es eine Bedingung, dass das Haus mit öffentlichen Verkehrsmitteln erreichbar war und es eine Einkaufsmöglichkeit in Gehdistanz des Hauses gab.

Fest stand, dass das Haus in der Region um Locarno, aber nicht südlicher davon sein sollte. Wir sahen uns verschiedene Liegenschaften in Tenero, Gordola und so weiter an, wurden aber nicht fündig. Von unseren Freunden in Brione erfuhren wir dann einmal, dass ein steiles, verwildertes Grundstück an der Via Panoramica zum Verkauf angeboten wurde. Meine Mutter kaufte es im Jahr 1968 von einer Familie aus Nidwalden für 60 000 Schweizer Franken. Bald

Abode

Fig. 56 Pergola / Pergola

In fact, Casa Kalman had two clients: Paula Kalman-Fränkel (1915–2016), a pediatrician in Zurich-Schwamendingen, and her daughter, Vera Brunner-Kalman, a lawyer and psychotherapist. In September 2021, the latter (VB) answered the following questions that were put to her by the author (HS) during a conversation about the Casa Kalman.[9]

9 Conversation in the Casa Kalman on 18.9.2021.

HS Why did your mother want to move to Ticino?
VB My maternal grandparents came from Cracow. They were honeymooning in Switzerland in 1914 when the First World War broke out and forced them to remain here. Although he had worked as a lawyer in Cracow my grandfather, Dr. Leon Fränkel, earned his living here by producing and selling fine leather goods. He was always proud of the fact that during the crises in the 1930s and 1940s he never had to let any of his workers go and always voted socialist. All his life he regretted that he did not own any real estate. Even though he worked in his own business he also did the bookkeeping for my mother, who worked as a pediatrician and was a single mother with all the difficulties that involves. He was therefore always fully informed about her financial situation.

As my grandmother had died while still relatively young, my mother looked after my grandfather and

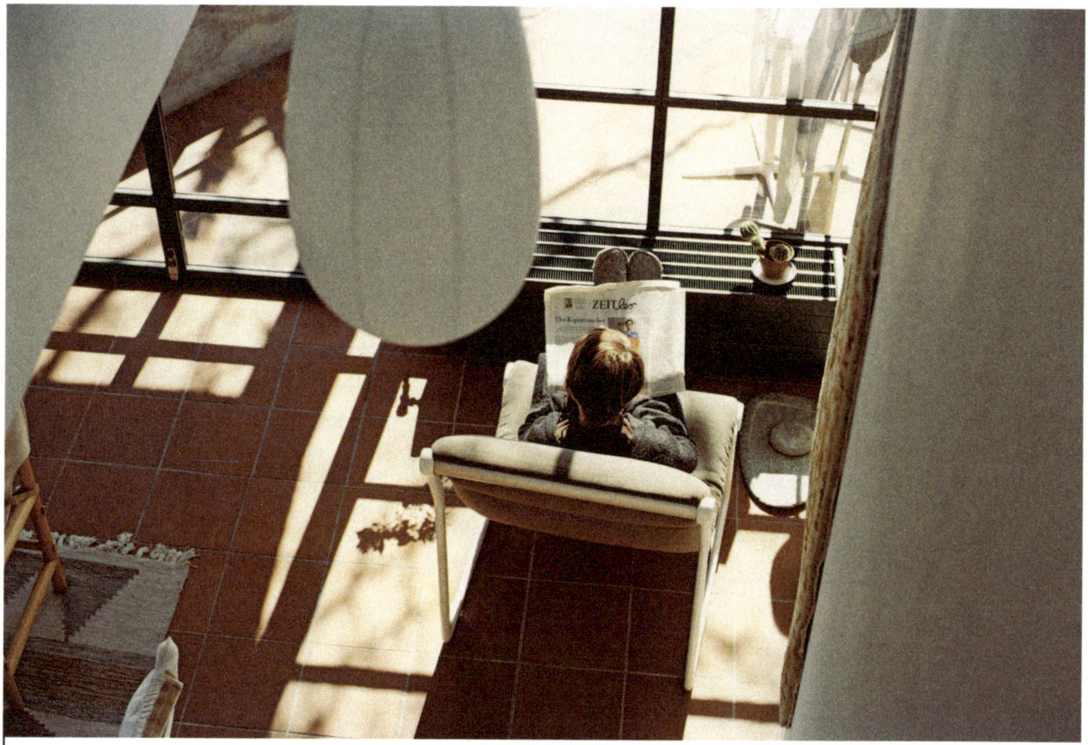

Fig. 57 Wohnzimmer vom Schlafgeschoss aus gesehen / Living room seen from the sleeping room floor

Fig. 58 Offener Kamin / Open fireplace

every year she spent the holidays with him in a house belonging to friends in Brione sopra Minusio. Their house was simple and in an ideal location and my mother was most impressed by it. This is where the idea of a holiday home in Ticino came from. It was my grandfather in particular who urged my mother to buy a holiday house. First of all, we considered where such a house might be found and then we started to look for houses that were for sale. My mother was a practical woman and one of her practical requirements was that it should be possible to reach the house by public transport and that there should be shops within walking distance.

It was decided that the house should be in the region around Locarno but not further south. We looked at various properties in Tenero, Gordola and so forth but found nothing suitable. Then we heard from our friends in Brione that a steep overgrown site on the Via Panoramica was for sale. In 1968 my mother bought it from a Nidwalden family for the sum of 60,000 Swiss Francs. A short time later I left to stay for two years in the United States of America. It was clear to my mother that she would not start to plan or to build during my absence.

HS   How did the story continue when you returned from the States?
VB   Initially, my mother thought that we should commission a building contractor, which was what our friends had done. However, I wanted good architecture of real quality and was able to persuade my mother. My brother-in-law had studied architecture at the ETH in Zurich and we asked him for a few recommendations. As he had worked for a long time abroad and didn't know anybody in Ticino, he asked one of his former fellow students who came from Ticino. This friend replied that he knew an architect, a certain Luigi Snozzi.

Vera Brunner-Kalman passed this name on to her mother, who then contacted Snozzi. In a letter from June 1973 Paula Kalman wrote to the architect: "Following our telephone conversation on 7.6. [June 7th], I would like to give you a brief description of, roughly, what I want. A simple but solid house, if possible, with 2 apartments. Downstairs 2 rooms, above 3–4 rooms (no 'captured'[10] rooms). Upper apartment with 3 rooms (possibly a fourth small room with bunk beds and closets), bathroom, a separate WC with shower, a small but well-fitted kitchen, if possible, with a door to a terrace, a balcony, seating area or similar. A fireplace is not required. A garage or parking space for car. Not a house for show but comfortable

[10] In German "gefangene Räume" (literally "captured rooms"). By this the client meant rooms that can only be entered through other rooms.

Wohnstatt

10
Dr. Paula Kalman an Luigi Snozzi. Brief vom 9.6.1973. Nachlass Luigi Snozzi, Archivio del Moderno, Balerna.

darauf bin ich für zwei Jahre in die Vereinigten Staaten von Amerika gegangen. Für meine Mutter war klar, dass sie in der Zeit meiner Abwesenheit nicht zu planen oder zu bauen beginnen würde.

HS Wie ging die Geschichte weiter, nachdem du aus den Staaten zurückgekommen warst?
VB Meine Mutter dachte zuerst, man könnte einen Baumeister beauftragen, so, wie unsere Freunde es gemacht hatten. Ich jedoch wollte eine ansprechende, gute Architektur, und meine Mutter liess sich überzeugen. Mein Schwager hatte an der ETH Architektur studiert und ihn habe ich um Empfehlungen gebeten. Da er lange Zeit im Ausland gearbeitet hatte und auch niemanden im Tessin kannte, fragte er einen seiner ehemaligen Tessiner Kommilitonen. Dieser antwortete, er würde einen kennen, einen gewissen Luigi Snozzi.

Vera Brunner-Kalman gab diesen Namen an ihre Mutter weiter und sie nahm Kontakt mit ihm auf. In einem Brief vom Juni 1973 schrieb Paula Kalman an den Architekten: „Als Fortsetzung unseres Telephongesprächs am 7.6. möchte ich Ihnen kurz schildern, was ich ungefähr wünsche. Einfaches, aber solides Haus, wenn möglich mit 2 Wohnungen. Unten 2, oben 3–4 Zimmer (keine ‚gefangenen' Zimmer), Wohnung oben: 3 Zimmer (ev. 4. kleines mit Kajütenbett u. Kästen), Bad, sep. WC mit Dusche, kleine, aber gut ausgebaute Küche, möglichst mit Ausgang auf Terrasse, Balkon, Sitzplatz oder dergleichen. Cheminée nicht nötig. Garage oder Abstellplatz für Auto. Kein Repräsentativbau, dafür gemütlich (also kein grosser ‚Wohnraum'). Das Haus sollte man auch im Alter allein besorgen und geniessen können, und ev. auch mit Rollstuhl zu gebrauchen sein. Es würde mich freuen, wenn wir darüber sprechen könnten, u. wenn ich bei dieser Gelegenheit etwas sehen könnte, was Sie gebaut haben."[10]

HS Was waren die Dinge, die für deine Mutter und dich im zukünftigen Ferienhaus wichtig waren?
VB Meine Mutter wünschte sich ein Haus für sich und ihre zwei Kinder. Auch, dass die Kinder später ihre eigenen Kinder mitbringen könnten und dass man das Haus auch im Alter benützen kann. Dass jedes Zimmer nicht nur als Schlafzimmer, sondern auch als Wohnraum benützt werden kann. Wichtig war ihr, dass die Treppen die richtigen Höhen hätten und dass die Türen nach aussen aufgehen sollten. Daraufhin stellte sie Snozzi die SIA-Normen zu, damit er sich daran hielte. Das Haus sollte sehr einfach, möglichst günstig zu errichten sein und das Terrain nicht viel Gartenarbeit beanspruchen.

(i.e., no large 'drawing room'). The house should be designed so that one can maintain it alone and enjoy it when one is older and, possibly, use it even if in a wheelchair. I would be very happy if we could talk about this and if I could have an opportunity to look at something you have already built."[11]

[11] Dr. Paula Kalman to Luigi Snozzi. Letter dated 9.6.1973. Estate of Luigi Snozzi, Archivio del Moderno, Balerna.

HS   What were the things that were important for your mother and for you in your future holiday house?

VB   My mother wanted a house for herself and her two children. And she wanted that the children could later bring their own children there and that one could use the house in one's old age. She wanted that every room could be used not just as a bedroom but also as a living room. It was important to her that the steps should be the proper height and that the doors should open outwards. She presented Snozzi with the SIA norms, so that he would adhere to them. The house was to be very simple, not expensive, and the grounds should not require too much gardening work.

The reason my mother wanted to be able to make two separate dwellings in the house was related to her experiences in Hungary. After the war we lived in Budapest, as my father, Dr. András Kálmán, was Hungarian. During a political show trial in 1949, he was sent to jail, where he died. Together with her children (I had an older brother) my mother was deported to Nyíregyháza in the east of Hungary, where we lived under numerous restrictions, closely monitored by the secret police. My mother was later rehabilitated and in 1956 she moved back to Switzerland with us children. She suffered constantly from the communist "trauma" and feared that the Russians would at some time or other conquer Switzerland. Therefore, it was important to her from the start that the house—if it were to be expropriated under communist rule—could be divided into two self-contained apartments. She always believed that this was a possible scenario. I had no ideas or wishes for the house; I was curious about the ideas and proposals that Snozzi brought with him to the meetings. I then responded to them.

According to Vera Brunner-Kalman between commissioning the architect in the second half of 1973 and the completion of construction work in spring 1976 there were around six person-to-person meetings between client and architect, all of which took place in Zurich. As Paula Kalman was a committed doctor with a busy schedule and Luigi Snozzi taught at the ETH in Zurich between 1973 and 1975, it was easiest for them to meet in Zurich.

Der Grund, warum meine Mutter die Möglichkeit zu zwei Wohneinheiten im Haus haben wollte, hängt mit ihren Erlebnissen in Ungarn zusammen. Nach dem Krieg lebten wir in Budapest, denn mein Vater, Dr. András Kálmán, war Ungar. Im Jahr 1949 kam er im Rahmen eines Säuberungsprozesses ins Gefängnis, wo er starb. Meine Mutter wurde mit ihren Kindern (ich hatte einen älteren Bruder) nach Nyíregyháza im Osten Ungarns deportiert, wo wir mit vielen Einschränkungen und unter strenger Aufsicht der Geheimpolizei lebten. Meine Mutter wurde später rehabilitiert und zog 1956 mit uns Kindern zurück in die Schweiz. Sie litt stets an dem kommunistischen „Trauma" und befürchtete, dass irgendwann die Russen auch die Schweiz erobern würden. Daher war ihr von Anfang an wichtig, dass das Haus – sofern es unter kommunistischer Herrschaft enteignet werden würde – in zwei autonome Wohnungen aufgeteilt werden könnte. Sie sah dies stets als ein mögliches Schreckensszenario. Ich selber hatte keine Vorstellungen und Wünsche an das Haus, ich war neugierig auf die Ideen und Vorschläge von Snozzi, die er zu den Besprechungen brachte. Auf die bin ich dann eingegangen.

Zwischen der Beauftragung in der zweiten Jahreshälfte 1973 und dem Bauende im Frühjahr 1976 gab es, laut Aussage von Vera Brunner-Kalman, etwa sechs persönliche Treffen, die allesamt in Zürich stattfanden. Da Paula Kalman eine engagierte Ärztin mit einem vollen Terminkalender war und Luigi Snozzi 1973 bis 1975 als Gastdozent an der ETH in Zürich unterrichtete, konnte er sich mit ihr einfach in Zürich für Besprechungen treffen.

HS Wie sah das erste Treffen zwischen Luigi Snozzi und euch aus?

VB Meine Mutter bereitete für Besuche meistens eine Fruchtwähe vor und bot Tee oder Kaffee an, das war auch bei Snozzi so. Sie fragte ihn, was er für eine Ausbildung durchlaufen und, ich glaube auch, ob er Familie hatte. Wichtig für sie war es auch zu fragen, für welche politische Überzeugung er eintrat. Er antwortete, dass er dem linken politischen Spektrum angehörte, dass er sich beim Heimatschutz engagierte und dass für ihn die Tessiner Tradition sehr wichtig sei – selbstverständlich auch beim Bauen.

Der Architekt wirkte sehr sympathisch, stets ein wenig nervös, weil er ständig rauchte und oft nach Worten rang. Wir sprachen nämlich immer Deutsch.

HS How was the first meeting between Luigi Snozzi and you and your mother?
VB My mother generally made a fruit tart for visitors and offered them tea or coffee, and this was what she prepared for Snozzi, too. She asked him about his education, and I think she also asked him if he had a family. It was important for her to enquire about his political convictions. He answered that he was on the left-wing of the political spectrum, that he was involved

Fig. 59 Wohnzimmer / Living room

Aus den Unterlagen geht hervor, dass Frau Kalman stets mit Forderungen für eine praktikable Benützung des Hauses ankam. So finden sich auf erhaltenen Blättern, die offenbar während dieser Projektbesprechungen entstanden sind, folgende Notizen: „Eingang WC nicht auf der Küche" oder „Treppen!!! Gemütlich wie möglich!".[11] Zwischenzeitlich versandte Paula Kalman Briefe mit Überlegungen an das Büro in Locarno und erhielt von dort Berichte, Rechnungen und verschiedene Planstände zugesandt.

Im Gespräch mit Vera Brunner-Kalman ist die Sprache auf eine Baustellenbesichtigung vonseiten der Bauherrinnen gekommen. Obschon es im Archiv einen Briefwechsel im Dezember 1975 und Januar 1976 für eine solche gibt, kann sich Vera Brunner-Kalman nicht daran erinnern.[12] Am ersten Weihnachtsfeiertag 1975 – da stand der Rohbau bereits in grossen Teilen – schrieb ihre Mutter an Luigi Snozzi: „Wir sind natürlich schrecklich gespannt u. freuen uns, weil Sie mir vor paar Wochen so begeistert telephoniert haben."[13]

[11] Undatierte Notizen. Nachlass Luigi Snozzi, Archivio del Moderno, Balerna.

[12] Brief von Dr. Paula Kalman an Luigi Snozzi vom 25.12.1975. Ankündigung Kalmans wegen einer Fahrt ins Tessin sowie Brief vom 15./17.1.1976. Darin ein Vorschlag Snozzis für eine Baustellenbegehung. Nachlass Luigi Snozzi, Archivio del Moderno, Balerna.

[13] Brief vom 25.12.1975, Dr. Paula Kalman an Luigi Snozzi. Nachlass Luigi Snozzi, Archivio del Moderno, Balerna.

HS   Welche Erinnerungen hast du an diese Besprechungen?

VB   Wir haben unterschiedliche Projektstände diskutiert und über Herausforderungen, die das Gelände dem Bau auferlegte, gesprochen. Aber auch über Detailfragen: So sagte meine Mutter zu Luigi Snozzi, als es um die Kücheneinrichtung ging: „Machen Sie es so, wie Sie es sich vorstellen, aber es sollte die günstigste Variante sein." Schliesslich hat er eine Forsterküche bestellt. Das Gleiche passierte dann bei der Wahl der Einrichtung der Bäder und der Kacheln für Küche und Bäder.

HS   Hast du ihr jemals Wohnmagazine als Referenzen gezeigt?

VB   Nein, nie. Es wurden keine Wünsche von mir in das Haus hineingetragen, ich habe immer nur gesagt, was mir nicht gefällt. Meine Mutter mochte das Haus unserer Freunde in Brione, das ein einfaches Haus an einem Hang aus der Feder eines Baumeisters war. Auf Eingangsebene eine grosse Stube, Küche, Balkon und WC, darunter vier kleine Schlafzimmer, zum Teil mit Stockbetten, und ein Bad. Sie wollte immer, dass Snozzi sich dieses ansieht, aber dazu kam es nie.

Am 10. Juni 1976 verliess ein Brief mit Schlüsseln das Büro Snozzi in Richtung Zürich. Die Adressatinnen machten sich daraufhin mit dem Auto auf den Weg ins Tessin und beäugten mit staunenden und nicht minder kritischen Blicken das neue Feriendomizil.

with the *Heimatschutz*, and that Ticino tradition was very important to him—naturally also as regards building.

The architect was very agreeable, he always seemed a little nervous, as he smoked constantly, and he often had to search for words, because we spoke German all the time.

The documents show that Mrs. Kalman always came to discussions with requirements to do with the practical use of the house. On surviving sheets of paper, the following notes, which seem to have been made during the discussions, can be found: "Entrance to WC not from the kitchen" or "stairs!!! As easy to climb as possible!"[12] Now and then Paula Kalman sent letters with her thoughts and ideas to the office in Locarno and from there she was sent reports, invoices, and details of the various stages of the planning.

While talking to Vera Brunner-Kalman the topic of site visits by the clients arose. Although in the archive there is correspondence about visits in December 1975 and January 1976, Vera Brunner-Kalman cannot remember one.[13] On the first day of the Christmas holidays 1975—when large parts of the building shell were already standing—her mother wrote to Luigi Snozzi: "We are naturally very excited and are delighted that you were so enthusiastic when you phoned me a few weeks ago."[14]

[12] Undated notes. Estate of Luigi Snozzi, Archivio del Moderno, Balerna.

[13] Letter from Dr. Paula Kalman to Luigi Snozzi dated 25.12.1975. Kalman's announces her intention to drive to Ticino, as well as letter from 15./17.1.1976. In it Snozzi suggests making a visit to the building site. Estate of Luigi Snozzi, Archivio del Moderno, Balerna.

[14] Letter dated 25.12.1975, Dr. Paula Kalman to Luigi Snozzi. Estate of Luigi Snozzi, Archivio del Moderno, Balerna.

HS   What are your memories of these meetings?
VB   We discussed the various stages of the project and talked about the challenges presented by the site. And about details, too: for instance, when they were talking about the kitchen fittings my mother said to Luigi Snozzi: "do it the way you imagine it, but it should be the most economical version." In the end he ordered a Forster kitchen. The same happened when choosing the bathroom fittings and the tiles for the kitchen and bathrooms.

HS   Did you ever show her an interior design magazine as a reference?
VB   No, never. No wishes of mine were incorporated in the house, I only always said what I didn't like. My mother liked our friends' house in Brione, which was a simple house on a slope, designed by a building contractor. On the entrance level there was a large living room, a kitchen, a balcony, and a WC, below there were four small bedrooms, some with bunkbeds, and a bathroom. She always wanted Snozzi to have a look at this house, but he never did.

Wohnstatt

Fig. 60 — Südfassade bei Nacht / South façade at night

Fig. 61 — Kellergeschoss / Basement floor

On June 10, 1976, a letter containing keys was sent from Snozzi's office to Zurich. Those to whom the letter was addressed then made their way by car to Ticino where they looked at their new holiday home with amazement but also a degree of criticism.

15
Dr. Paula Kalman to Luigi Snozzi. Letter dated 24.5.1976. Estate of Luigi Snozzi, Archivio del Moderno, Balerna.

HS   What was it like when you saw the house for the first time?

VB   My mother and I arrived at the house, Snozzi was not there. We drove a Renault R4, and we brought two folding beds for us and one for my daughter who was one year old. We looked at the house, my mother was very disappointed. The first thing she immediately disliked on looking at the house was the huge TV aerial on the roof. Snozzi simply had this mounted because at the time a TV aerial was one of the basic fittings for a house in Ticino. My mother did not want a TV in the first place, and she disliked the aerial both for aesthetic reasons and because it was pointless. She was unhappy with the openness of the rooms and the fact that sound traveled so easily through the house. She was a very practically-minded person and she immediately considered how these defects might be remedied and how the openings could be walled up. For a long time, she was not happy with the house.

In a letter describing her first reactions to the new house the client begins most politely: "Dear Mr. Snozzi, I can hardly tell you how much Vera and I liked the house. Every corner, every view is interesting. We are convinced that you have extracted the most possible from this slope that is inclined on three sides, from this difficult terrain. I am particularly happy that you write that you have come to love your work. My wish is that my family and, hopefully, I too, will feel well in this house for many years." After this initial praise she does not hold back with her complaints and expresses her dissatisfaction directly: "Dear Mr. Snozzi please allow me to make a few critical comments. These have nothing to do with the architecture, as I understand little about that, but with external things where I feel my wishes have been ignored. As already mentioned, the TV system which, as far as I am concerned could have been fitted during the construction work, but without an aerial. Then the WC downstairs and the bathroom upstairs: it is true I wanted a house without luxury, a house that is 'cheap' but also practical and beautiful. The two wash-hand basins should be somewhat bigger. The toilet bowls should be the kind that are mounted on the walls, not ones from the previous century or ones that have been left-over from somewhere. I do not think I am being petty in criticizing these things, I find they are like blemishes on a beautiful picture."[15]

14
Dr. Paula Kalman an Luigi Snozzi. Brief vom 24.5.1976. Nachlass Luigi Snozzi, Archivio del Moderno, Balerna.

HS Wie war es dann, als ihr das Haus das erste Mal gesehen habt?

VB Meine Mutter und ich sind zum Haus gekommen, Snozzi war nicht dabei. Wir hatten einen Renault R4 und zwei Klappbetten für uns und eines für meine einjährige Tochter mitgenommen. Wir haben das Haus angeschaut und meine Mutter war sehr enttäuscht. Beim Anblick des Hauses missfiel ihr sofort die riesige Fernsehantenne auf dem Dach. Snozzi hatte diese einfach aufstellen lassen, weil das damals im Tessin zur Grundausstattung gehörte. Aus ästhetischen Gründen wie auch wegen der Nutzlosigkeit – meine Mutter wollte keinen Fernseher – war ihr diese zuwider. Darüber hinaus störte sie besonders die Offenheit der Zimmer und die Hellhörigkeit im ganzen Haus. Sie war ein sehr praktisch veranlagter Mensch und hat sofort überlegt, wie man diese Makel beheben und die Öffnungen zumauern könnte. Sie war lange mit dem Haus nicht zufrieden.

Diplomatisch begann die Bauherrin in einem ersten Reaktionsschreiben auf das neue Haus: „Lieber Herr Snozzi, Ich kann Ihnen gar nicht beschreiben, wie mir und Vera das Haus gefallen hat. Jede Ecke, jeder Ausblick ist interessant. Wir sind überzeugt, dass Sie auf diesem Abhang mit seinen Neigungen auf drei Seiten, mit diesem schlechten Boden das Bestmögliche herausgearbeitet haben. Und was mich besonders beglückt, ist Ihre Aussage, dass Sie Ihr Werk liebgewonnen haben. Mein Wunsch ist, dass sich meine Familie und hoffentlich ich selber auch noch einige Jahre im Haus wohl fühlen werden." Neben dieser Würdigung hielt sie ihre Beanstandungen nicht zurück und präsentierte ihm unverhohlen ihr Missfallen: „Lieber Herr Snozzi, erlauben Sie, dass ich doch noch mit einer Kritik herausrücke. Die Kritik betrifft nicht die Architektonik, denn da sehe ich und verstehe zu wenig, sondern Äusserlichkeiten, bei denen ich mich nun tatsächlich übergangen fühle. Wie schon erwähnt, die Fernsehanlage, die man meinetwegen beim Bau schon hätte einrichten können, aber ohne Antenne. Dann das WC unten und das Badezimmer oben: es ist schon richtig: ich habe es ohne Luxus gewünscht, also ‚billig', aber auch praktisch und schön. Die beiden Waschbecken hätten etwas grösser sein dürfen. Die Abortschüsseln an der Wand hängend und nicht solche vom letzten Jahrhundert oder ‚Ladenhüter'. Ich fühle mich nicht ‚kleinlich', wenn ich diese Sachen bemängle, sondern ich empfinde sie als Flecken auf einem schönen Bild."[14]

HS Im Planungsprozess habt ihr euch ja irgendwann auf einen Entwurf geeinigt, der umgesetzt werden würde. Da sah man doch bereits, wie das Haus und die Räume aussehen würden. Hat sie da nicht widersprochen?

Fig. 62 — Pergola / Pergola

HS During the planning process there must have been a point at which you agreed on a design, which was then implemented. This design would have already shown how the house and the rooms would look. Why did she not object then?

VB Snozzi always communicated his plans very well. He was a very enthusiastic person, and he was able to convince me completely. I assume that at the time I understood the plans, but perhaps my mother didn't. At the meetings he always made sketches, mostly of the views that one would have from different points in the house.

Although she did not like the house initially, she allowed it to take effect on her and in time she became accustomed to it. When it was acclaimed internationally, she began to truly accept the house and eventually she liked it very much indeed.

Over its lifetime, the exterior of the house has undergone several changes —some of them quite incisive. In the 1980s the house was connected to the public drainage system and the wall along the east façade, behind which the septic tank had been located, was taken down. The antenna on the flat roof was only removed after the start of the new millennium.

VB Seine Pläne hat er stets gut kommuniziert. Snozzi war ein sehr begeisterungsfähiger Mensch, und in meinem Fall konnte er mich wirklich für seine Pläne begeistern. Ich nehme an, dass ich damals die Pläne verstanden habe, meine Mutter vielleicht nicht. Er hat bei den Besprechungen immer wieder Skizzen angefertigt, vor allem von den Perspektiven, die man von den verschiedenen Orten im Haus hat.

Auch wenn ihr das Haus anfangs nicht behagte, hat sie sich darauf eingelassen und sich mit der Zeit daran gewöhnt. Als dann die weltweite Anerkennung kam, begann sie sich wirklich mit dem Haus auszusöhnen und mochte es sehr gerne.

Aussen erfuhr das Haus im Laufe seines Bestehens einige – teils einschneidende – Veränderungen. So wurde es in den 1980er-Jahren an das Kanalisationsnetz angeschlossen, woraufhin man die Mauer entlang der Ostfassade, hinter der sich die Senkgrube befand, rückbaute. Erst nach der Jahrtausendwende wurde die Antenne vom Flachdach entfernt.

HS Welche Veränderungen gab es im Laufe der Zeit?
VB Es gab keine wesentlichen Veränderungen, wir haben sehr sorgfältig auf das Haus geachtet. Wie bei anderen Häusern auch mussten wir die Heizung erneuern und haben die Fensterscheiben – aber nicht die Rahmen – ausgetauscht.

HS Jedes Mal fallen mir, wenn ich zum Wohngeschoss die Treppe hochgehe, diese Spiegelfliesen auf.
VB Die sind von Ikea. Sie haben mir gefallen und ich dachte, sie würden passen. Es gab keinen anständigen Spiegel im Haus. Das ist mein Spiegel.

Heute steht die Casa Kalman, umgeben von Häusern aus den letzten sechs, sieben Jahrzehnten, da wie ein besonderer Solitär. Sie besticht durch ihr brutalistisches Erscheinungsbild, ihre uniforme Materialität und ihre aussergewöhnliche Form. Den vorbeiziehenden Spaziergängerinnen und Wandersleuten mögen Assoziationen von Bunkerbauten in den Sinn kommen.

HS Wie lebt es sich in diesem Haus?
VB Ich fühle mich so wohl. Auch wenn es tagelang regnet, fühle ich mich wirklich wohl. Es hat auch damit zu tun, dass das Haus so hell ist. Ich habe nicht das Bedürfnis, aus dem Haus rauszugehen, zu wandern oder etwas zu unternehmen. Es ist ein einfaches Haus, diese Einfachheit ist meiner Mutter zu verdanken.

Abode

Fig. 63 — Ausblick aus dem Wohnzimmer / View from the living room

Fig. 64 — Brunnen in der Pergola / Fountain in the Pergola

Fig. 65 Schrägansicht von Nordost / Oblique view from northeast

Und es ist ein praktisches, leicht zu unterhaltendes Haus. Als ich noch gearbeitet habe, bin ich oftmals nur für eine Nacht oder für ein Wochenende ins Haus gekommen. Nachher hatte ich das Gefühl, als ob ich in den Ferien gewesen wäre.
    Das Haus war und ist ein Ferienhaus. Es hat uns immer leidgetan, dass wir das Haus nicht öfter und dauerhafter genutzt haben.

HS Wo sind deine Lieblingsplätze im Haus?
VB Meist auf dem Sofa in der Stube mit Ausblick auf die Pergola und in der Ferne den See. Wenn es draussen heiss ist, gehe ich nicht raus, da bin ich die meiste Zeit im Haus. Wenn ich Gäste habe, sitzen wir gerne unter der Pergola auf der Terrasse, bei einem nicht enden wollenden Frühstück.

HS Wie seid ihr mit dieser steilen Hanglage zurechtgekommen?
VB Meine Mutter ist nie aufs Grundstück gegangen. Sie ist zwar gerne gewandert, fühlte sich aber immer unsicher. Ich bin gerne draussen, habe auch mehrjährige Blumen, Pflanzen und Kräuter gepflanzt.

HS   What changes have been made over the course of time?
VB   There have been no major changes, we have always taken loving care of the house. As is the case with many houses we had to renew the heating system and we replaced the windows—but using the same frames.

HS   Every time I climb the stairs up to the living room floor, I notice the mirror tiles.
VB   They are from IKEA. I liked them and thought they would be suitable. There is no proper mirror in the house. They are my mirror.

Today, surrounded by houses from the past six or seven decades, the Casa Kalman stands there like a special freestanding building. Its brutalist appearance, its uniform materiality, and its unusual form make it stand out. For people strolling by and ramblers it may call to mind a bunker.

HS   What is it like to live in this building?
VB   I feel well there. Even if it rains for days, I feel extremely well. This probably has to do with the fact that the house is so bright. I don't feel any need to leave the house to go for a walk or to undertake something. It is a simple house, this simplicity is thanks to my mother, and it is a practical house, easy to maintain. When I was still working, I often came to the house for a night or a weekend. Afterwards I felt as if I had been on holiday.
    The house was and is a holiday home. We were always sorry that we did not use it more often and for longer periods.

HS   What are your favorite places in the house?
VB   Generally, sitting on the sofa in the living room with a view of the pergola and the lake in the distance. When it is hot, I don't go outside, I spend most of the time inside the house. When I have guests, we like to sit on the terrace under the pergola and enjoy a breakfast that goes on forever.

HS   How did you cope with the steep slope on the site?
VB   My mother never walked around the grounds. Although she liked to ramble, she always felt unsafe there. I like to be outdoors, and I have planted perennial flowers, other plants, and herbs. Leaving the meadow in a natural state is practical, as it means

Wegen der Naturwiese ist es praktisch, dass man wenig anpflanzen und selten mähen muss.

HS Wieso trägt das Haus den Namen Casa Kalman?
VB Das ist fremdbenannt. Mit der Publizität wurde es recht bald Casa Kalman genannt. Das kam entweder von Snozzi selbst oder von den Architekturpublikationen. Meine Mutter wollte jedoch, dass es Casa Vera heisst.

Fig. 66 — Terrasse sowie West- und Südfassade / Terrace, west and south façade

you don't have to do much planting, and it doesn't have to be mowed very often.

HS How come the house is called Casa Kalman?
VB It was given that name by others. Through the publicity it came to be known as the Casa Kalman at an early stage. This name came either from Snozzi himself or from the architecture journals. My mother wanted it to be called Casa Vera.

Fig. 67 Terrasse und Pergola vom Wohnzimmer aus / Terrace and pergola from the living room

| Fig. 68 „Kalmann (sic!) House", Zeitschrift *a+u. architecture and urbanism*, Nr. 69, Tokyo 1976, S. 60–61/ "Kalmann (sic!) House", magazine *a+u. architecture and urbanism*, No. 69, Tokyo 1976, pp. 60–61

Der Casa Kalman wohnt ein Mythos inne, dessen Urheber Luigi Snozzi selbst war. Es bedarf dafür eines Blicks in die mediale Produktion rund um das Haus. Im Nachlass von Luigi Snozzi befindet sich ein Typoskript in deutscher Sprache aus dem Jahr 1976, das eine Beschreibung der Casa Kalman wiedergibt. Dieser Text diente als Grundlage für Beiträge in Fachzeitschriften.

15
Kalmann House. In: *a+u. architecture and urbanism.* Nr. 69, Tokyo 1976, S. 60–65.

Die Septemberausgabe 1976 der international vertriebenen japanischen Zeitschrift *a+u. architecture and urbanism*[15] widmete sich der neuesten Schweizer Architektur. Darin präsentierte man unter dem Titel „Kalmann house" (sic!) das noch in Bau befindliche Ferienhaus. |Fig. 68| Die Fotografien von Alberto Flammer zeigen einen Rohbauzustand, bei dem die Fensterrahmen noch keine Scheiben aufweisen und rund um das Haus noch Baustellentreiben herrscht. Obschon zum Zeitpunkt der Publikation das Haus fertiggestellt und übergeben war, musste für die Drucklegung bereits im Frühjahr 1976 Bild- und Textmaterial an die Redaktion in Japan geschickt werden. |Fig. 69| Der kurze ins Englische übersetzte Begleittext basiert auf dem Text des Typoskripts. Der Schweizer Architekturöffentlichkeit

Myth

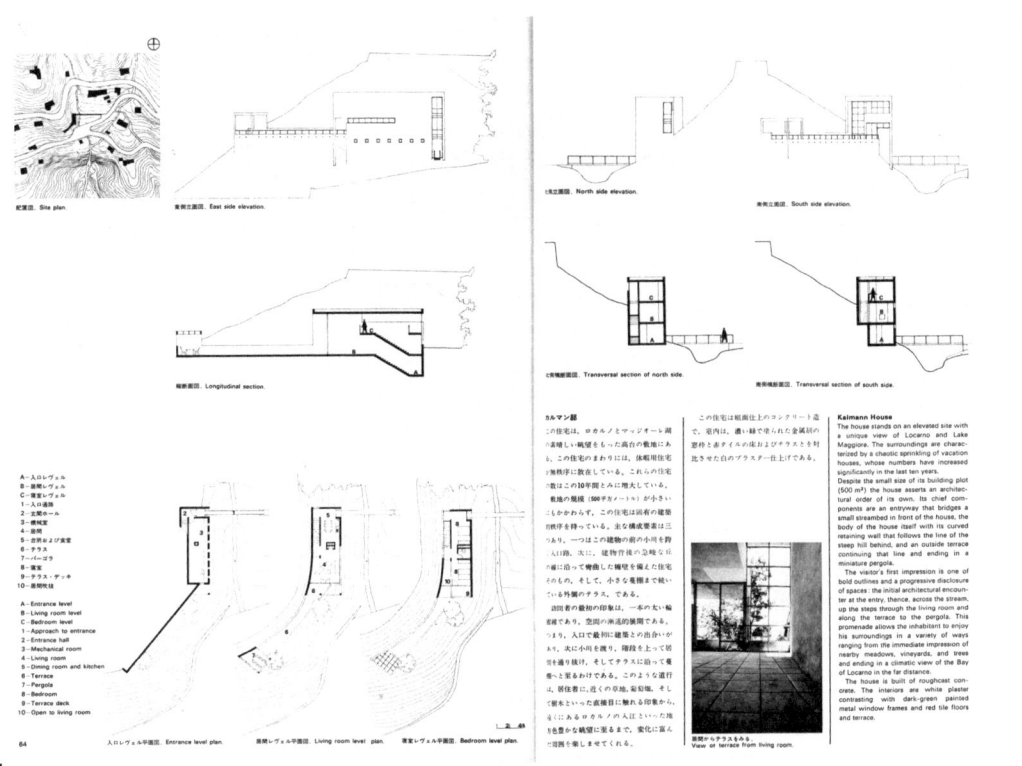

Fig. 69 | „Kalmann (sic!) House", Zeitschrift *a+u. architecture and urbanism*, Nr. 69, Tokyo 1976, S. 64–65 / "Kalmann (sic!) House", magazine *a+u. architecture and urbanism*, No. 69, Tokyo 1976, pp. 64–65

The Casa Kalman is surrounded by a kind of myth that Luigi Snozzi himself created. To describe it, we need to look at the media production about this house. Among the papers of Luigi Snozzi there is a typoscript in German dating from 1976 that provides a description of the Casa Kalman. This text provided a basis for contributions to specialist journals.

16
Kalmann House. In: *a+u. architecture and urbanism*. No. 69, Tokyo 1976, pp. 60–65.

The September 1976 issue of the internationally circulated Japanese magazine *a+u. architecture and urbanism* was devoted to recent Swiss architecture.[16] The holiday home, which was still under construction at the time, was presented under the title "Kalmann House" (sic). | Fig. 68 | The photographs by Alberto Flammer show the building shell in which there is not yet any glazing in the window frames and there are obvious signs of ongoing construction work around the outside of the house. Although by the time the magazine was published the house had been completed and handed over, to meet printing deadlines the texts and photographic material had to be sent to the editing office in Japan in spring. | Fig. 69 | The short accompanying text that was translated into English was based on the typoscript text. In contrast the completed building was presented

wurde hingegen das fertiggestellte Bauwerk ein Jahr später in der Septemberausgabe 1977 der renommierten Schweizer Architekturzeitschrift *werk archithese*[16] vorgestellt. Mit dem Titel *Zwei Wohnhäuser im Tessin* wurden unter der Rubrik „Bauchronik" das „Wohnhaus Kalman" und die „Wohnhäuser Bianchetti" vorgestellt. | Fig. 70 | Der Text stammte von Luigi Snozzi selbst und ist eine leicht erweiterte Variante des erhaltenen Typoskripts. In der Dezemberausgabe 1977 der ebenso respektablen Zeitschrift *rivista tecnica della Svizzera italiana*[17] wurde der vollständige Text des Typoskriptes ins Italienische übertragen und abgedruckt.

Für die Mai/Juni-Ausgabe 1984 der Zeitschrift *archithese*, die dem Thema „Ort/Lieu" gewidmet war, verfasste Luigi Snozzi einen längeren Beitrag in italienischer Sprache, der jedoch – übersetzt von Heinrich Helfenstein – auch in Deutsch abgedruckt wurde. Damit sich sein Text im übergeordneten Heftthema wiederfindet, übertitelte er ihn mit „Il luogo o la ricerca del silenzio / Der Ort oder die Suche nach der Stille".[18] Darin beschreibt er am Beispiel der Casa Kalman seine Bedenken am Anfang der Beauftragung, wie er den Kontext bewertete und schliesslich die Qualitäten des Ortes zu lesen, zu erkennen und zu schätzen begann. „Der geografisch durch eine Folge von Geländerücken und Bachtobeln charakterisierte Hügel ist bis zur Unkenntlichkeit entstellt. Ein Teil der Bäche wurde kanalisiert und eingedeckt. Stützmauern jeder Art, Dimension und Richtung schaffen horizontale Landstücke für Häuser und Swimming Pools. Im Ganzen ein Chaos, ein Durcheinander von Bauformen."[19] Die Auftaktillustration zeigt eine Collage aus vier Fotografien, die das leere Grundstück mit dem ehemaligen Bewuchs zeigen.

Die französische Architekturzeitschrift *AA Architecture d'aujourd'hui* verwies in ihrem Dezemberheft desselben Jahres auf diesen Beitrag und schaltete eine Doppelseite über den Tessiner Architekten.[20] Luigi Snozzi verfasste einen kurzen neuen Text unter dem Titel „Promenade Architectural"[21], und wieder zog er die Casa Kalman für seine Argumentation heran. Im Herbst desselben Jahres würdigte man Luigi Snozzi mit einer monografischen Ausstellung im Architekturmuseum Basel, zu der eine deutsch-italienische Publikation erschien.[22] Realisierte Arbeiten genauso wie Zeichnung gebliebene Projekte von 1957 bis 1984 wurden gezeigt und publiziert, selbstverständlich auch

---

16
D. P., Zwei Wohnhäuser im Tessin. In: *werk archithese. Zeitschrift und Schriftenreihe für Architektur und Kunst.* Heft 9, Jg. 64, Zürich 1977, S. 55–58, darin: Snozzi, Luigi: Wohnhaus Kalman, S. 56–57.

17
S[nozzi]., L[uigi].: Casa a Locarno-Brione. In: *rivista tecnica della Svizzera italiana.* Nr. 12, Lugano 1977, S. 18–20. Dabei handelte es sich um den gleichen – nur ins Italienische übersetzten – Artikel.

18
Snozzi, Luigi: Il luogo o la ricerca del silenzio / Der Ort oder die Suche nach der Stille. In: *archithese. Zeitschrift und Schriftenreihe für Architektur und Kunst.* Heft 3–84, Jg. 14, Zürich 1984, S. 23–27, 32.

19
Snozzi, Luigi: Il luogo o la ricerca del silenzio / Der Ort oder die Suche nach der Stille. In: *archithese. Zeitschrift und Schriftenreihe für Architektur und Kunst.* Heft 3–84, Jg. 14, Zürich 1984, S. 23.

20
Snozzi, Luigi: Promenade Architecturale. In: *Architecture aujourdhui.* Nr. 236, Paris 1984, S. 34–35.

21
Snozzi, Luigi: Promenade Architecturale. In: *Architecture aujourdhui.* Nr. 236, Paris 1984, S. 34–35.

22
Croset, Pierre-Alain (Red.): *Luigi Snozzi. Progetti e architetture. 1957–1984.* Milano 1984, S. 44/45.

Bauchronik

der Identifizierung der Architekturelemente in Evidenz gebracht. Gerade der bewusst gesuchte Kontrast zur umliegenden baulichen Struktur mittels einer sachlichen Architektur trägt zur Qualifizierung der Manifestation bei. Die Analogie zur architektonischen Sprache des «Neuen Bauens» ist evident, und zwar positiv gemeint, denn Snozzis Bezugnahme ist nicht an bekannten kompositorischen Themen der Modernen Bewegung, sondern an der Sachlichkeit der Formulierung von Elementen und deren räumlichen Zusammenhängen sowie an der ihnen übertragenen Bedeutung lesbar. Dadurch weist die Architektur Signifikanten auf, die als Instrumente zum Erkennen des vom Objekt gebildeten Ortes aufgefasst werden können.

Diese Bauten zeigen uns zwei Aspekte in der jüngsten Entwicklung der Architektur Luigi Snozzis: die Anlehnung an die Leistungen der Mitglieder der 1926 gegründeten «Gruppe 7», später MIAR (Movimento italiano per l'architettura razionale) genannt, und den Beweis einer nochmals erfolgten Analyse des Werkes Le Corbusiers, wie die subtilere und reifere Interpretation einiger Entwurfscharakteristiken des Meisters erkennen lässt. Zu der zweiten Bemerkung möchten wir die Thematik des «Parcours» als gedankliches und formales Gerüst des architektonischen Systems besonders hervorheben. Der Parcours, die Führung zum und im «Ort», ist bei den Beispielen Snozzis – vor allem im Haus Dr. Bianchetti – der wertvollste Signifikant seiner Intervention. Wir fassen dies als die intellektuelle Komponente im architektonischen Denkprozess Luigi Snozzis auf.

Zu den Beispielen

Die hier präsentierten Privathäuser Dr. Kalman in Brione s. Minusio und Dr. Bianchetti in Orselina stellen die neuesten Realisierungen des Architekten Luigi Snozzi dar. Wir haben beide Objekte ausgewählt mit der Absicht, die Rigorosität der Entwurfsarbeit und die konsequente Haltung des Tessiner Architekten, die seinem «Denken und Handeln, also auch dem Entwerfen zugrunde liegt, welche jede konsumistische, utilitaristische und effizientistische Absicht der gegenwärtigen Gesellschaft ablehnt»*, ans Licht zu bringen. In diesem Verhalten erkennt man das politische Engagement, aus dem der Architekt Luigi Snozzi eine seiner Entwurfsmotivationen gewinnt.

Beide Häuser liegen auf fast gleicher Höhe in derselben Landschaft oberhalb des Seeteils vor Muralto und Locarno: am dicht bebauten Südhang der Monti di Cardada, durch viele enge Täler intensiv und differenziert strukturiert.

D.P.

* Luigi Snozzi, «Entwurfsmotivationen», in *Tendenzen. Neuere Architektur im Tessin*, Dokumentation zur Ausstellung an der ETH Zürich vom 20. November bis 13. Dezember 1975, zusammengestellt durch Martin Steinmann und Thomas Boga. ETH Z Organisationsstelle für Ausstellungen des Institutes GTA.

Wohnhaus Kalman
in Brione über Minusio

Architekt: Luigi Snozzi, Locarno
Mitarbeiter: Walter von Euw
Ingenieur: Peppino Bondietti, Locarno
Baujahr: 1976
Fotos: Alberto Flammer, Locarno

Das kleine Wohnhaus – Wohnraum und zwei Schlafzimmer – wurde auf einem extrem kleinen Grundstück (ca. 500 m²) mit starker Neigung erbaut. Die ungeordnete Ansammlung von kitschigen Ferienhäusern, hauptsächlich in den letzten 10 Jahren entstanden, kennzeichnen die Umgebung.

Diese Art Aufgabe stellt in unserer Praxis wohl den häufigsten Fall dar. Ich denke, dass es auch in solch schwierigen Fällen noch möglich ist, einige wichtige Entwurfsanliegen auszudrücken. Es wurde versucht, die geografischen Werte des Ortes (den Hang, das Tälchen, den kleinen Bach) mit dem Entwurf aufzuwerten, da sie meist ignoriert und zerstört werden. Der Bach wird oft in unterirdische Kanäle verbannt, die Topographie wird mittels riesiger Stützmauern, Abgrabungen und Auffüllungen zerstört. Ich versuchte, das Haus als eine neue ordnende Struktur des umgebenden Territoriums zu entwerfen, mit dem Willen, die Landschaft neu zu zeichnen und zu definieren. Dieser Versuch lässt erahnen, was die öffentlichen Gebäude für die «neue»

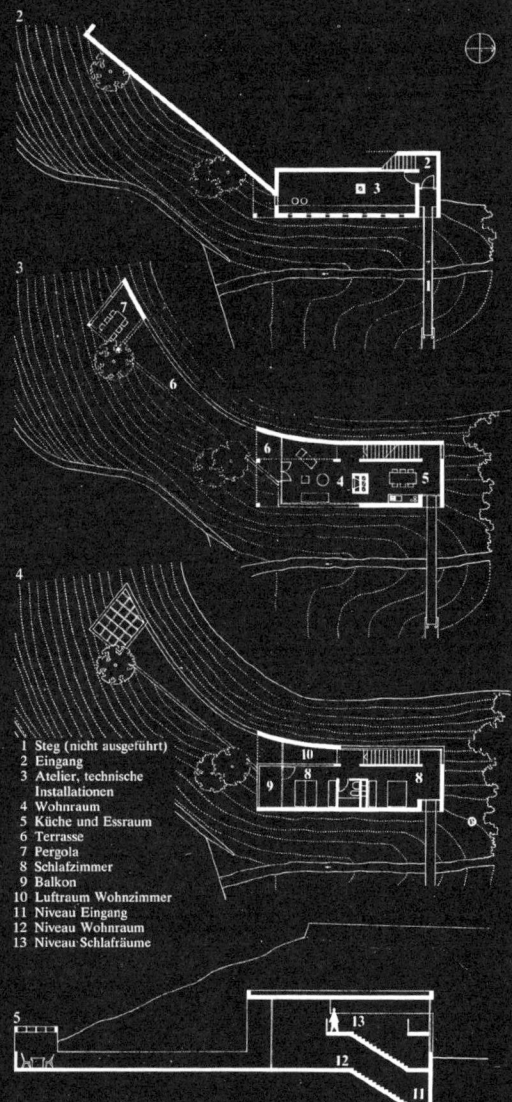

1 Steg (nicht ausgeführt)
2 Eingang
3 Atelier, technische Installationen
4 Wohnraum
5 Küche und Essraum
6 Terrasse
7 Pergola
8 Schlafzimmer
9 Balkon
10 Luftraum Wohnzimmer
11 Niveau Eingang
12 Niveau Wohnraum
13 Niveau Schlafräume

2 *Grundriss Eingangsgeschoss. Der geplante Zugang mit Steg vom nebenliegenden Terrain kam nicht zur Ausführung. Zum Eingang gelangt man nun über einen zum Haus parallelen, abgetreppten Weg, welcher an der tiefer liegenden Strasse beginnt*
3 *Grundriss Wohngeschoss*
4 *Grundriss Schlafgeschoss*
5 *Längsschnitt*
6 *Querschnitt*

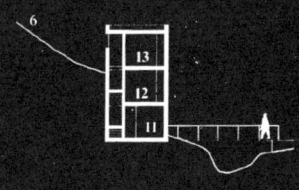

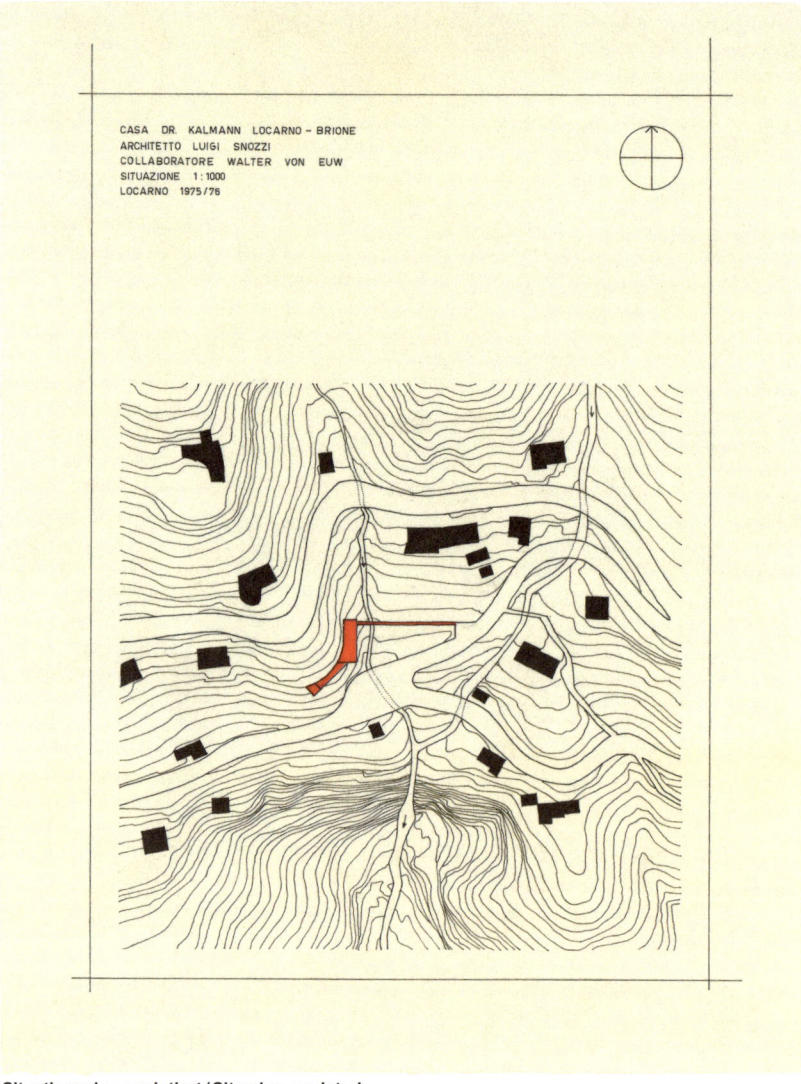

Fig. 71 Situationsplan, undatiert / Site plan, undated

die Casa Kalman. Da innerhalb des Büros der Name der Bauherrin über die Jahre hinweg mit „Kalmann" geführt wurde, passierte es, dass in dieser Publikation der Name auch so geschrieben wurde. Der Fehler hat sich vervielfältigt, denn in den sozialen Medien und Bildplattformen im World Wide Web finden sich Treffer sowohl mit der richtigen als auch mit der falschen Schreibweise.

In allen oben genannten Publikationen wird ein Mythos durch eine gezielte mediale Strategie kreiert. Den Texten, die er entweder selbst schrieb oder die von anderen Autorinnen und Autoren verfasst wurden, fügte der Architekt eigens dafür zu verwendendes

to the Swiss architecture public one year later in the September 1977 issue of the prestigious Swiss architecture journal *werk archithese*[17]. The "Wohnhaus Kalman" and the "Wohnhäuser Bianchetti" were published in the section "Bauchronik", under the title "Zwei Wohnhäuser im Tessin" (Two Houses in Ticino). |Fig.70| The text was by Luigi Snozzi and is a slightly longer version of the typoscript. A translation into Italian of the entire typoscript was printed in the December 1977 issue of the equally prestigious journal *rivista tecnica della Svizzera italiana.*[18]

For the May/June 1984 issue of the magazine *archithese*, which was dedicated to the theme "Ort/Lieu" (Place), Luigi Snozzi wrote a longer contribution in Italian, which was also published in German—in a translation by Heinrich Helfenstein. So that his text would reflect the magazine's main theme, he gave it the title "Il luogo o la ricerca del silenzio/Der Ort oder die Suche nach der Stille" (The Place or the Search for Silence).[19] Using the example of the Casa Kalman he describes his initial reservations when he first received the commission, how he evaluated the context and how he finally began to recognize and appreciate the qualities of the place. "The hill, which in geographic terms is

[17] D. P., Zwei Wohnhäuser im Tessin. In: *werk archithese. Zeitschrift und Schriftenreihe für Architektur und Kunst.* Issue 9, vol. 64, Zurich 1977, pp. 55–58, with: Snozzi, Luigi: Wohnhaus Kalman, pp. 56–57.

[18] S[nozzi]., L[uigi].: Casa a Locarno-Brione. In: *rivista tecnica della Svizzera italiana.* No. 12, Lugano 1977, pp. 18–20. This is the same article but translated into Italian.

[19] Snozzi, Luigi: Il luogo o la ricerca del silenzio/Der Ort oder die Suche nach der Stille. In: *archithese. Zeitschrift und Schriftenreihe für Architektur und Kunst.* Issue 3–84, vol. 14, Zurich 1984, pp. 23–27, 32.

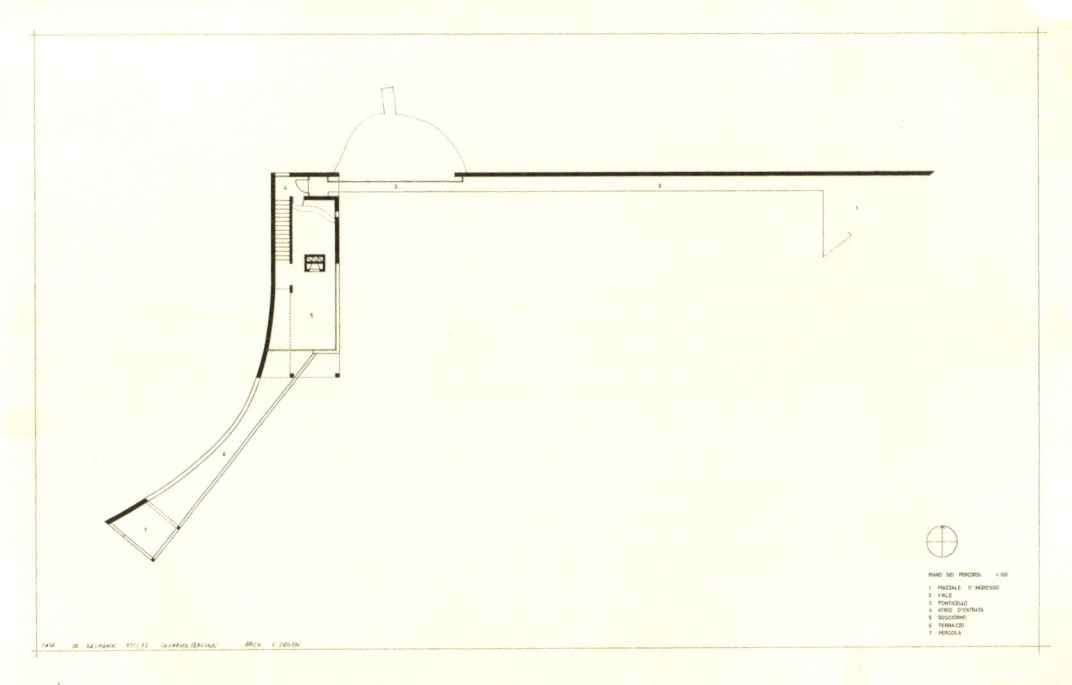

|Fig. 72| Grundrissplan des Zuganges und des Wohngeschosses, undatiert / Floor plan of the access and the living room floor, undated

[23] Snozzi, Luigi: Wohnhaus Kalman. In: *werk archithese. Zeitschrift und Schriftenreihe für Architektur und Kunst.* Heft 9, Jg. 64, Zürich 1977, S. 56.

[24] Museum für Gestaltung (Hg.) / Steiger, Bruno (Red.): *Luigi Snozzi. Auf den Spuren des Ortes*. Schriftenreihe / Museum für Gestaltung Zürich 21, Zürich: Eigenverlag von Schule und Museum für Gestaltung 1996.

[25] Lichtenstein, Claude: *Luigi Snozzi*. Basel / Boston / Berlin: Birkhäuser 1997, S. 52–57.

Planmaterial von der Casa Kalman bei. |Fig. 71/72| Dabei zeigte Snozzi ausschliesslich seine bevorzugte, idealisierte Vorstellung des Hauses. Im Übrigen eine gängige Praxis im Architekturbetrieb, man denke nur an die *I quattro libri dell'architettura* (1570) von Andrea Palladio, die ein Kompendium von Idealprojekten darstellen. In Snozzis Idealvorstellung besticht zum einen die besondere Zugangssituation: Von einem kleinen Autoabstellplatz im Osten führt ein ebener, gerader Weg exakt in Ost-West-Richtung orthogonal auf das Haus zu. Nach einer kleinen Brücke über den Bachlauf erreicht er schliesslich den gedeckten Eingangsbereich des Hauses. Zum anderen im Inneren: Die Grundrisse des Keller- und des Wohngeschosses sind schlicht und offen. In den oben erwähnten Artikeln zwischen 1977 und 1984 wird immer wieder auf die idealisierte „promenade architecturale" hingewiesen. Dafür ist es essenziell, das fiktive Projekt zu zeigen, da es in seiner stringenten Konzeption das ausgeführte Projekt bei Weitem überragt.

    Snozzis Idee einer besonders ausgeklügelten Wegführung, einer inszenierten Annäherung und Querung des Hauses findet sich bereits im allerersten Projekt vom Winter 1973. Dessen Apotheose feierte er jedoch in seinem nicht realisierten Idealprojekt der Casa Kalman, das nur als Zeichnung vorliegt. Da das Grundstück, auf dem sich der Autostellplatz und die Brücke hätten befinden sollen, zu keiner Zeit der Besitzerin der Casa Kalman gehörte, notierte er auch: „Der gesamte Zugang mit Steg vom nebenliegenden Terrain kam nicht zur Ausführung."[23] Im tatsächlich ausgeführten Eingangsbereich sticht eine Sache ins Auge: Die Bodenplatte vor dem Eingang ist nicht Teil der Bodenplatte des Hauses. Hingegen weist sie zu den Seitenwänden einen Abstand von etwa 16 cm auf. Mit dieser Geste weist Snozzi im realisierten Bau auf sein geliebtes Idealprojekt hin. Sie ist der Torso des Steges, den er nie ausführen konnte. |Fig. 20/21|

    Auch in späteren Publikationen über das Haus finden sich die von Snozzi bevorzugten Pläne. Erst 1996 und 1997 werden Pläne, die mehr den ausgeführten Zuständen entsprechen, gezeigt. In der Ausstellung im Museum für Gestaltung in Zürich 1996[24] sowie in der umfassenden Publikation von Claude Lichtenstein[25] werden zwei Projektstände – aus den Archivbeständen des Büros – publiziert, nämlich jene vom Juni 1974 und vom Januar 1975.

[20] Snozzi, Luigi: Il luogo o la ricerca del silenzio / Der Ort oder die Suche nach der Stille. In: *archithese. Zeitschrift und Schriftenreihe für Architektur und Kunst*. Issue 3–84, vol. 14, Zurich 1984, p. 23.

[21] Snozzi, Luigi: Promenade Architecturale. In: *Architecture aujourdhui*. No. 236, Paris 1984, pp. 34–35.

[22] Snozzi, Luigi: Promenade Architecturale. In: *Architecture aujourdhui*. No. 236, Paris 1984, pp. 34–35.

[23] Croset, Pierre-Alain (Red.): *Luigi Snozzi. Progetti e architetture. 1957–1984*. Milano 1984, pp. 44/45.

characterized by a series of ridges and creeks, has been disfigured beyond recognition. Some of the streams have been culverted and covered over. Retaining walls of all kinds, sizes and directions create flat, horizontal sites for houses and swimming pools."[20] The first illustration is a collage of four photographs that show the empty site with the original vegetation.

In its December issue of the same year the French architecture magazine *AA Architecture d'aujourd'hui* referred to this contribution and printed a double page about the Ticino architect.[21] Luigi Snozzi wrote a short new text under the title "Promenade Architecturale"[22], and again used the example of the Casa Kalman for his argumentation. In the autumn of the same year Luigi Snozzi was honored with a monograph exhibition in the Architecture Museum Basel, which was accompanied by a publication in German and Italian.[23] Built works as well as projects that never went further than the drawing board from between 1957 and 1984 were shown and published, including, of course, the Casa Kalman. Because for years the client's name had been written in the office as "Kalmann", it was also spelt in this way in the publication. This mistake has multiplied, and on social media and picture platforms in the Internet hits can be found using both the correct and incorrect spelling.

In all the publications mentioned above a myth was created by means of a calculated media strategy. The architect added plan material about the Casa Kalman made specifically for this purpose to texts that he wrote himself or that were produced by other authors. | Figs. 71/72 | Snozzi showed only his preferred, idealized impression of the house. This is widespread practice in the world of architecture, here one thinks of, for instance, the *I quattro libri dell'architettura* (1570) by Andrea Palladio, which is a compendium of ideal projects. In Snozzi's ideal presentation what stands out is, firstly, the special approach situation: from a small parking place in the east a level, straight path leads precisely in an east-west direction at right angles to the house. After crossing a small bridge over a stream, the route finally arrives at the covered entrance area to the house. A second striking aspect is the interior: the floorplans of the basement and living room floor are simple and open. In the articles mentioned above, which were written between 1977 and 1984, repeated reference is made to an idealized "promenade architecturale".

Jedoch, das Ideal wurde nicht nur publizistisch vervielfältigt. Als man im Architekturbüro das Neubauprojekt für das Nebengrundstück im Jahr 2005 zu planen begann, verwendete man in den internen Projektplänen weiterhin den Idealzustand der Casa Kalman.

Darüber hinaus kam und kommt es durch die Proliferation der Bilder in den sozialen Medien zu einer steten Wiederholung dieses idealen Projektstandes. Auf institutionellen und privaten Seiten im World Wide Web sowie auf den einschlägigen Bildplattformen finden sich zuhauf hochgeladene Bilder der Casa Kalman – selbst produzierte oder aus der Literatur reproduzierte – und auch Planmaterial des Idealprojekts.

Die schiere Menge an Publikationen über die Casa Kalman im Idealzustand ebenso wie die zahlreichen Bilder davon in den unterschiedlichen digitalen Medien befördern weiterhin diesen vor vielen Jahren in die Welt gesetzten Mythos. In der antiken Theorie stand dem Mythos der Logos gegenüber. Während der eine den Anspruch auf Geltung für eine von ihm behauptete Wahrheit erhebt, versucht der andere durch rationale Beweise die Wahrheit seiner Behauptungen zu begründen. Ähnlich scheint es sich mit den beiden Realitäten der Casa Kalman zu verhalten: Snozzis mythische Wahrheit auf der einen Seite und die gebaute Wahrheit auf der anderen Seite.

Während seiner Lehrtätigkeit als Gastprofessor an der ETH Zürich in den 1970er-Jahren formulierte Luigi Snozzi seine Aphorismen zur Architektur, die durch ihre berückende Brisanz und Aktualität nichts von ihrer ursprünglichen intellektuellen Wucht eingebüsst haben. Snozzi war es vollkommen bewusst, dass er mit jedwedem baulichen Eingriff die „Natur" respektive „Landschaft" veränderte, mehr noch, dass er sie zerstörte. „Jeder Eingriff bedingt eine Zerstörung: zerstöre mit Verstand!" ist wohl der meistzitierte der insgesamt 25 Aphorismen.[26] Die vorgefundene „Natur" wird verändert, und für ihn war eine Veränderung nur dann zulässig, wenn sie auch zu einer Aufwertung sowie einer symbiotischen Verschränkung von Vorgefundenem und Neuem führte. Snozzi ist es mittels der Casa Kalman gelungen, diese Verbindung zu schaffen und zeichenhaft die Schönheit und den Reichtum des als unbebaubar taxierten Terrains mittels einer aussergewöhnlichen Architektur vor Augen zu führen.[27]

---

[26] Hierbei handelt es sich um die ältere Version dieses Aphorismus aus „Unser architektonisches Brevier", das im Büro Snozzi in den 1970er-Jahren entstand. Für die Entstehungsgeschichte, die genaue Anzahl und die neu formulierten Aphorismen siehe: Rimmel, Maximilian / Edition Bibliothek Werner Oechslin (Hg.): *Luigi Snozzi. 25 Aphorismen zur Architektur.* Basel: Schwabe Verlag 2013.

[27] Das Lebenswerk von Luigi Snozzi. www.youtube.com/watch?v=la-I0yXt9-Q (abgerufen am 18.2.2022).

[24] Snozzi, Luigi: Wohnhaus Kalman. In: *werk archithese. Zeitschrift und Schriftenreihe für Architektur und Kunst*. Issue 9, vol. 64, Zurich 1977, p. 56.

[25] Museum für Gestaltung (ed.) / Steiger, Bruno (Red.): *Luigi Snozzi. Auf den Spuren des Ortes*. Schriftenreihe / Museum für Gestaltung Zurich 21, Zürich: Eigenverlag von Schule und Museum für Gestaltung 1996.

[26] Lichtenstein, Claude: *Luigi Snozzi*. Basel / Boston / Berlin: Birkhäuser 1997, pp. 52–57.

To illustrate this, it is essential to show the fictive project, as it is far more conceptually stringent than the design that was built in the end.

Snozzi's idea of a carefully considered route, a staged approach to the house and a path through it, is already evident in the very first project dated winter 1973. However, he celebrates its apotheosis in his ideal project for the Casa Kalman, which was not realized and exists only as a drawing. As the site where the car parking space and the bridge were to be made never belonged to the owner of the Casa Kalman, he noted: "The entire approach with a footbridge from the adjoining terrain was never carried out."[24] In the entrance area as made one aspect attracts your attention: the ground slab in front of the entrance does not form part of the floor slab of the house. On the contrary: on either side there is a gap of about 16 cm between the ground slab and the side walls. This gesture by Snozzi in the building as realized is a reference to his beloved ideal project. It is the torso of the footbridge that he was never able to build. |Figs. 20/21|

Later publications about the house also feature the plans that Snozzi preferred. It was only in 1996 and 1997 that plans were shown which more closely resembled the house as actually built. In the exhibition held in the Museum für Gestaltung Zurich in 1996[25] and in the comprehensive publication by Claude Lichtenstein[26] two versions of the project—from the office archive—were published, a version dated June 1974 and one from January 1975.

It was not just in publications that this ideal was disseminated; in 2005, when plans were being drawn up in the office for a new building on the neighboring site, the ideal version of the Casa Kalman was used to depict the existing building.

Additionally, through the proliferation of images in the social media, this ideal version of the project has been used repeatedly. On institutional and private Internet sites and on the relevant image platforms there are numerous uploaded images of the Casa Kalman —self-produced or reproduced from the literature— as well as plans of the ideal project.

The sheer number of publications about the ideal version of the Casa Kalman as well as the many pictures of it in various digital media also support the myth created many years ago. In the theory of classical antiquity, myth is contrasted with logos. While the former

Die Art und Weise, wie die Casa Kalman auf dem Grundstück positioniert wurde, bedingte grosse Erdarbeiten. Diese Eingriffe bilden sich im Verlauf der winkeligen Gesamtkomposition von Haus und Terrasse sowie der gebogenen Stütz- und der geraden Terrassenmauer eindrücklich ab. Die Dramatik der Setzung und die präzise Orientierung des Wohnhauses nutzte Snozzi sowohl für das Bild, das er mit dem Haus innerhalb der gebauten Umwelt kreieren wollte, als auch für die Exemplifizierung wichtiger architektonischer Themen. Die Casa Kalman ist ein architektonischer Katalysator, durch den wesentliche Aufgabenstellungen der Architektur vergegenwärtigt werden.

Das Bauen entstand aus der Notwendigkeit heraus, sich gegen die Unbilden der Natur zu schützen. Der gesamte bauliche Komplex steht an einem Steilhang und fungiert als Schutzwand für das Haus selbst, aber auch für das Terrain. Der gebogene Verlauf der Hangmauer war für Snozzi auch die materialisierte Nobilitierung der Qualitäten dieses Ortes.

Die Wände im Westen, Norden und Osten sind durch hohe vertikale und lange horizontale Fenster sowie durch Einzelfenster gegliedert. Die Fassaden im Verband mit dem beschotterten Flachdach – in der Errichtungszeit eher eine Ausnahmeerscheinung im Tessin – verbildlichen die Konzeption einer robusten Hülle für ein zu schützendes Inneres. Gänzlich geöffnet ist hingegen die Südfassade. Einige Skizzen aus der frühen Entstehungszeit zeugen bereits von dieser Idee. Die Disposition des Innenraumes, der Verglasung mit Tür und Fenster sowie des Ausblicks lassen an das Landhaus Khuner (1928–1930) von Adolf Loos denken, der eine wichtige Referenz für Luigi Snozzi war. |Fig.73| In den frühen Planstufen war es gedacht, dass sich etwa über dem Hauseingang ein wesentlich höherer Raum befindet, der nach Norden hin durch eine zusätzliche Öffnung eine Querung für Licht und Luft bereitstellt. Ebenso war angedacht, die Westseite mit einer sehr grossen Öffnung zu versehen, die eine ähnliche Querung vom Nordende der Terrasse auf das Grundstück bereitstellt. Diese poröse Qualität des Baukörpers, die im Laufe des Planungsprozesses zugunsten einer kompakteren Lösung aufgegeben wurde, findet sich jedoch in der beinahe zeitgleich errichteten Casa Bianchetti in Locarno-Monti.

Die Ausgestaltung der Wände – innen wie aussen – hat sich in materieller Hinsicht ebenso im Verlauf der

Myth

Fig. 73 — Ausblick aus dem Wohnzimmer / View from the living room

claims the validity of a truth it asserts, the latter attempts to establish the truth of its assertions by means of rational evidence. As regards the two realities of the Casa Kalman things seem much the same: Snozzi's mythical truth on the one hand, the built reality on the other.

While teaching as a guest professor at the ETH Zurich in the 1970s Luigi Snozzi formulated his aphorisms about architecture, which thanks to their captivating

Fig. 74 Ausblick aus dem Wohnzimmer / View from the living room
Fig. 75 Ecksituation im nördlichen Schlafzimmer / Corner situation in the northern bedroom

28 Typoskript. Nachlass Snozzi, Archivio del Moderno, Balerna, sowie: Snozzi, Luigi: Wohnhaus Kalman. In: *werk archithese. Zeitschrift und Schriftenreihe für Architektur und Kunst*. Heft 9, Jg. 64, Zürich 1977, S. 58.

Evolution des Projektes verändert. Baustoffe wie Naturstein, Holz und Klinker waren für die Fassadengestaltung vorgesehen. Heute stellt sich das Ferienhaus mit einer rauen Schale aus Sichtbeton dar, die zwar keinen allzu weichen, aber doch gemütlichen Kern umschliesst. Das Innere besticht durch lediglich zwei Hauptfarben: Wände und Decken sind weiss gestrichen, der Boden besteht aus typisch rostbraunen Terrakottaplatten, über die Snozzi schreibt: „… und alle Fussböden der Zimmer und der Aussenterrasse [sind] mit roten Tonplatten belegt. Diese Platten bilden das wichtigste chromatische Element des Hauses."[28] Als dritte konzeptionelle Farbe dient dunkelgrün, mit welcher man sämtliche Geländer, metallenen Fenster- und Türrahmen sowie einige Türblätter anstrich. Blickt man von innen nach aussen, ergeben die grünen Fensterrahmen zur umgebenden Landschaft nur einen geringen Kontrast. | Fig. 74–76 | Ursprünglich gab es in den beiden Schlafzimmern einfache Industrieteppichböden, die vor wenigen Jahren durch dunkelbraune Linoleumböden ersetzt wurden. Schlicht

topicality and explosiveness have lost nothing of their original intellectual force. Snozzi was fully aware that with every built intervention he changed *nature* or *landscape* or even destroyed them. "Every intervention causes destruction: destroy reasonably!" is probably the most often quoted of the 25 aphorisms.[27] The existing *nature* is changed and for him change was acceptable only if it also leads to an enhancement and to a symbiotic intertwining of the existing and the new. With the Casa Kalman Snozzi succeeded in this kind of intertwining and by means of the exceptional quality of his architecture he also succeeded in revealing the beauty and richness of a terrain that had been regarded as impossible to build on.[28]

The way in which the Casa Kalman was placed on the site necessitated major earthworks. These interventions are shown by the angled composition of house and terrace and by the curved retaining wall and the straight terrace wall. Snozzi used the dramatic way the building is positioned and its precise orientation to create the image that he wanted of the house in its built surroundings, and also to exemplify important architectural themes. The Casa Kalman is an architectural catalyst by means of which fundamental tasks of architecture are identified.

Building developed from the need to protect oneself against the rigors of nature. The entire built complex stands on a steep slope and functions as a protective wall for the house itself, but also for the terrain. For Snozzi the curved line of the retaining wall also acknowledges and ennobles the topographical quality of the place and gives it material form.

The walls in the west, north and east are articulated by tall upright windows and long horizontal ones, as well as by single windows. These façades together with the gravel-covered flat roof—at the time it was built something exceptional in Ticino—illustrate the concept of a robust shell enclosing an interior that needs to be protected. In contrast, the south façade is completely open. A few sketches from the early design period already testify to this idea. The layout of the interior, the spacing of the glazing bars in the door and windows, and the view recall the Landhaus Khuner (1928–1930) by Adolf Loos, who was an important reference for Luigi Snozzi. | Fig. 73 | In the early planning stages it was intended that there should be a considerably higher space above the house entrance, which was to have an

---

[27] This is the older version of this aphorism from *Unser architektonisches Brevier*, which was written in Snozzi's office in the 1970s. For the history of how they were written, the exact number and the newly formulated aphorisms see: Rimmel, Maximilian / Edition Bibliothek Werner Oechslin (ed.): *Luigi Snozzi. 25 Aphorismen zur Architektur*. Basel: Schwabe Verlag 2013.

[28] Luigi Snozzi's lifework. www.youtube.com/watch?v=la-l0yXt9-Q (downloaded on 18.2.2022).

Mythos

29 Man meint hier, das Ideal Filaretes vom Haus der Tugend und des Lasters aus seinem *Trattato d'architettura* umgesetzt vor sich zu haben, wo er den Aufstieg über Treppen in die Höhe als den Weg zur Erleuchtung beschreibt.

Fig. 76 Bandfenster im Schlafgeschoss / Ribbon window on the bedroom floor

sind die Kacheln in den Bädern und der Küche gehalten: Sie sind weiss an den Wänden und schwarz am Badezimmerboden.

Schliesslich kommt noch ein immaterieller Aspekt zum Tragen, der durch den Weg und die Öffnungen, die den monolithischen Betonbau unterbrechen, bestimmt wird. Einerseits sind es die Lichtstimmungen, die durch die Setzung der Fenster orchestriert werden. Andererseits die Möglichkeiten an Ausblicken, die nicht minder kompositorisch behandelt sind, damit sich die Personen im Haus in Verbindung mit der umgebenden Landschaft setzen können. Beim Aufstieg über die beiden Treppen, die nach Süden führen, strebt man dabei den immer heller werdenden Bereichen im Haus zu.[29] Bereits beim Hochgehen der untersten Treppe auf das Wohngeschoss erahnt man den zweigeschossigen Luftraum im Wohnzimmer und sein helles Strahlen. Durch den Balkon im Schlafzimmergeschoss kommt es im Sommer zu einer Beschattung des Wohnzimmers, im Winter hingegen gelangen die Sonnenstrahlen bis zum offenen Kamin. Die ursprünglich geplante eingehängte Stahltreppe hätte dieser metaphysischen wie sensorischen Konzeption gleichermassen zuarbeiten

additional opening that would allow light and air to pass through to the north. It was also intended to make a very large opening on the west side, which would have created a similar crossing from the northern end of the terrace to the site. The porous quality of the building, which, as the design work advanced, was abandoned in favor of a more compact solution, is found in the Casa Bianchetti in Locarno-Monti, which was built at almost exactly the same time.

As the project evolved the design of the walls—inside and outside—changed in terms of material, too. Originally, materials like real stone, wood and clinker brick were envisaged for the façades. Today the holiday house has a rough shell of exposed concrete that encloses a core which, although not particularly soft, is nevertheless comfortable. Only two main colors are used in the interior: the walls and ceilings are painted white, while the floors are made of typical rusty brown terracotta slabs about which Snozzi writes: "… and all the floors in the rooms and the outdoor terrace are covered with red clay slabs. These slabs form the most important chromatic element of the house."[29] The third conceptual color is dark green, which was used to paint all the railings, metal window and door frames, and for a number of the doors. If you look outside from the interior, the green window frames contrast only slightly with the surrounding landscape. |Figs. 74–76| Originally there was industrial carpeting in both bedrooms, but it was replaced by dark brown linoleum a few years ago. The tiles in the bathrooms and kitchen are plain: white on the walls and black on the bathroom floor.

Finally, an immaterial aspect comes into play, which is determined by the route and the openings that interrupt the monolithic concrete building: on the one hand it is the moods of light that are orchestrated by the positioning of the windows, on the other the possibilities of views, which are composed so that people in the building can connect to the surrounding landscape. As you climb either of the two staircases, both of which lead southwards, you move towards increasingly bright parts of the house.[30] When climbing the stairs towards the living room floor you already experience the two-story void in the living room and its bright radiance. In summer, the balcony on the bedroom floor casts a shadow in the living room, whereas in winter the sunbeams penetrate as far as the open fireplace. The steel staircase originally planned was intended to contribute

---

[29] Typoscript. Estate of Snozzi, Archivio del Moderno, Balerna, as well as: Snozzi, Luigi: Wohnhaus Kalman. In: *werk archithese. Zeitschrift und Schriftenreihe für Architektur und Kunst*. Issue 9, vol. 64, Zürich 1977, p. 58.

[30] One could believe that one is confronted here with Filarete's ideal from the "House of Virtue and of Vice" in his Trattato d'architettura, in which he describes climbing staircases as the path to enlightenment.

sollen. Oben angelangt, blickt man durch das Bandfenster in der Ostwand auf das Bergpanorama am Ostufer des Lago Maggiore sowie auf die mächtigen Bäume. Bewegt man sich im Wohnzimmer weiter, fällt der Blick alsbald auf die Terrasse bis hin zu deren architektonischem Ende, der Pergola. Das raumhohe Fenster in der Küche – direkt über dem Eingangsbereich – und das darüberliegende Fenster im nördlichen Schlafzimmer orientieren sich nach Osten. Von hier aus kann man Gäste, die zum Haus kommen, sehen oder den Blick von der Magadinoebene bis hin zum Bergpanorama schweifen lassen. Bei gutem Wetter erhellt die Morgensonne mit ihrem warmen Licht diese beiden Räume. Wichtig war es für Snozzi und von Euw, dass beide Schlafzimmer eine Blickbeziehung zum See erhalten. Was für das Hauptschlafzimmer im Süden einfach zu erreichen war, schien für das nördliche beinahe unmöglich. Durch den Kunstgriff, in der nordwestlichen Ecke eine als innenliegenden Balkon ausgebildete Plattform zu errichten, stellten beide eine Ausblickmöglichkeit Richtung See her. |Fig. 77/78|

Fig. 77 — Räumliche Ausstülpung aus dem nördlichen Schlafzimmer / Spatial extension of the northern bedroom

to this metaphysical and sensory conception. Having arrived upstairs, you look through the ribbon window in the east wall at the mountain panorama along the eastern shore of Lago Maggiore and at the majestic trees. As you move further through the living room your gaze meets the terrace and the pergola that terminates it in architectural terms. The full-height window in the kitchen —directly above the entrance area—and the window

Fig. 78 — Ausblick von der Ausstülpung des nördlichen Schlafzimmers / View from the spatial extension of the northern bedroom

Fig. 79   Blick zur Pergola und zum See / View towards the pergola and the lake

above it in the northern bedroom both face east. From here you can see guests approaching the house or your gaze can roam from the Magadino Plain to the mountain panorama. If the weather is good the warm light of the morning sun brightens both these rooms. It was important to Snozzi und von Euw that both bedrooms should have a view of the lake. As regards the main bedroom in the south this was easily achieved but it seemed almost impossible for the northern one. Through the device of making a platform in the north-western corner that is a kind of internal balcony they created the possibility of a view towards the lake. |Figs. 77/78|

About halfway along the 15-meter-long terrace the retaining wall on the uphill side curves closer to the straight wall on the downhill side, reducing the width of the terrace to 1.4 meters, from there it curves away again so that at the far end the terrace is about 5 meters wide. The motif of tension and relaxation is celebrated not just spatially but also visually. You feel almost magically drawn towards the pergola, as you walk there a promising tension builds up. |Fig. 79| Once you stand in the pergola this tension is dissolved in the most positive possible way. By means of the framing the human being is grounded in the surroundings and is in harmony with the view of the lake and the trees. On the side facing up the slope the pergola consists of a wall, while on the downhill side it has two columns. |Fig. 80| The wall and columns are connected by concrete beams. As well as wire cables that provide support for vines there are two hooks for a children's swing. "This is the real window of the building, from where you can enjoy an overwhelming panorama that includes the entire town, the lake and the mountains."[31] Snozzi also describes the pergola's function as a visual reference element. Through it the high mountains of the surrounding landscape are captured in the foreground, their size is made relative, and they are reduced to a scale that viewers can relate to.[32] Through the arrangement of the volumes, the orientation, and the sensitive orchestration of the route and the openings the Casa Kalman invites those who use it to employ the house as a kind of subtle viewing machine. It builds up a system of skillfully staged points of reference that makes its positioning understandable and introduces a sense of scale into the project that can be understood at several levels. Through this contextual charging the house is ideally suited to the place, the landscape, and to the people who live in it.

[31] Croset, Pierre-Alain (ed.): *Luigi Snozzi. Progetti e architetture. 1957–1984*. Milano: Electa 1984, p. 44.

[32] Luigi Snozzi's life work. www.youtube.com/watch?v=la-I0yXt9-Q (retrieved on 18.2.2022).

30 Croset, Pierre-Alain (Red.): *Luigi Snozzi. Progetti e architetture. 1957–1984.* Milano: Electa 1984, S. 44.

31 Das Lebenswerk von Luigi Snozzi. www.youtube.com/watch?v=la-l0yXt9-Q (abgerufen am 18.2.2022).

Was die 15 m lange Terrasse anbelangt, so ergeben die gebogene Stützmauer auf der Hangseite und die gerade Mauer auf der Talseite nach etwa halber Strecke eine Verengung auf 1,4 m, die sich an deren Ende wieder auf etwa 5 m aufweitet. Das Motiv der Spannung und Entspannung wird aber nicht nur räumlich, sondern auch visuell zelebriert. Man wird wie magisch von der Pergola angezogen, auf dem Weg dorthin baut sich eine verheissungsvolle Spannung auf. |Fig. 79| Steht man in der Pergola, wird diese Spannung auf positivste Weise aufgelöst. Mittels der Rahmung ist der Mensch in der Umgebung verortet und im Einklang mit dem Ausblick auf See und Berge. Die Pergola besteht auf der Hangseite aus einer Wand und auf der Stützmauerseite aus zwei Stützen. |Fig. 80| Wand und Stützen sind alle durch Betonbalken verbunden. Neben Drahtseilen, die den Bewuchs mit Wein unterstützen, gibt es zwei Haken für das Aufhängen einer Kinderschaukel. „Dies ist das wirkliche Fenster des Gebäudes, von dem aus man ein überwältigendes Panorama, das die gesamte Stadt, den See und die Berge umfasst, geniessen kann."[30] Darüber hinaus beschreibt Snozzi die Funktion der Pergola als visuelles Bezugselement. Durch sie werden die hohen Berge der umgebenden Landschaft im Vordergrund gefasst, in ihrer Grösse relativiert und auf einen Massstab gebracht, mit dem die Betrachterinnen und Betrachter etwas anfangen können.[31] Die Casa Kalman lädt mit ihrer volumetrischen Disposition, ihrer Orientierung und ihrer feinsinnigen Orchestrierung des Weges und der Öffnungen die Benutzenden ein, sie als subtile Blickmaschine zu verwenden. Sie schafft es, ein System an verschiedenen, gekonnt inszenierten Bezugspunkten aufzubauen, das ihre Verortung sinnfällig macht und eine Massstäblichkeit ins Projekt bringt, die auf mehreren Ebenen nachvollziehbar wird. Durch die kontextuelle Aufladung wird sie dem Ort, der Landschaft sowie den Menschen, die sie bewohnen, in höchstem Masse gerecht.

Fig. 80 Detail der Pergola / Detail of the pergola

Ivo Bösch mutmasste in einem Interview mit Luigi Snozzi 2011, dass wohl jeder Architekturstudierende der Schweiz – und dies mag noch erweitert werden um jene aus vielen anderen Ländern – die Casa Kalman während des Studiums kennengelernt und vielleicht auch besichtigt hat. In besagtem Gespräch erzählte Luigi Snozzi davon, dass er sogar Modelle des Hauses Kalman in so manchen Schulen angetroffen hatte.[32]

[32] Das Lebenswerk von Luigi Snozzi. www.youtube.com/watch?v=la-l0yXt9-Q (abgerufen am 18.2.2022).

[33] Solothurner Schule, Stuttgarter Schule, Grazer Schule etc.

Was für die Referenz innerhalb der Ausbildungsstätten gilt, kann auch auf übergeordneter Ebene eingebettet werden. „Tessiner Schule", „Neue Tessiner Architektur", „Tendenzen" sind Bezeichnungen, mit denen versucht wurde, eine Gemeinsamkeit im Schaffen der Planenden im Tessin von den 1960er- bis zu den 1990er-Jahren auf einen gemeinsamen Nenner zu bringen. Labels wie diese werden zur leichteren Ein- und Zuordnung sowie zur besseren Subsumierung unter ein vages Image gerne geschaffen.[33] Nach der Ausstellung an der ETH Zürich *Tendenzen – Neuere Architektur im Tessin* von Martin Steinmann 1975 wurde der Begriff der „Tessiner Schule" von Kenneth Frampton 1978 geprägt. Die Rechnung ist aufgegangen. Die Interpretationen, die fern der Epizentren der eigentlichen Bautätigkeit angestellt wurden, kreierten eine *must see*-Architektur für Architektur-Aficionados sowie einen veritablen Exportschlager. Neben der Realisierung zahlreicher Bauten im Tessin von Architekten wie Mario Botta, Tita Carloni, Aurelio Galfetti, Livio Vacchini und der Architektin Flora Ruchat-Roncati sowie mehreren anderen erhielten viele von ihnen nationale wie internationale Aufträge. Die Tessiner Bauten stehen auf den Reiseplänen von Architektur-, Kultur- oder Studienreisen, die Bauwerke von Luigi Snozzi zählen dabei zu den fixen Stationen.

Neben den bisher dargelegten Themen und Rahmenbedingungen, die eine Baukultur einer Zeit ausmachen, seien an dieser Stelle weitere Aspekte genannt, die für das bessere Verständnis von Baukultur von Interesse sein könnten.

Bis vor wenigen Jahren lag im Büro Snozzi ein Schlüssel der Casa Kalman. Jedes Mal, wenn es eine Anfrage für eine Besichtigung des Hauses gab, konnte man mit Luigi Snozzi selbst oder einem seiner Mitarbeiter – selbstverständlich nach Absprache mit der Besitzerin – das Haus in Augenschein nehmen. Aufgrund seiner Bekanntheit war und ist der Anreiz für eine Besichtigung gross, und so haben bis heute viele Hundertschaften an Architekturaffinen das Bauwerk in eigener Anschauung erleben können.

Building culture

33
Luigi Snozzi's life work.
www.youtube.com/
watch?v=la-l0yXt9-Q
(retrieved on 15.2.2022).

34
Solothurner Schule,
Stuttgarter Schule,
Grazer Schule etc.

Fig. 81 Besichtigung des Büros Trinkler Stula Achille Architekten, Basel, 2021 /
Visit of the architecture office Trinkler Stula Achille Architekten, Basel, 2021

In an interview with Luigi Snozzi that he made in 2011 Ivo Bösch suggested that probably every architecture student in Switzerland got to know this house during their studies and possibly also visited it—the same is presumably true of many students from other countries. During this conversation Luigi Snozzi recounted how he had come across models of the Casa Kalman in several schools of architecture.[33]

What is true of the reference among the educational institutions can also be embedded at a higher level: "Ticino School", "New Ticino Architecture", "Tendencies" are all terms that represent an attempt to find a common denominator for the creative work of planners in Ticino from the 1960s to the 1990s. Labels such as these are frequently used to help classify and attribute buildings and to subsume them under a vague image.[34] Following the exhibition *Tendenzen – Neuere Architektur im Tessin* by Martin Steinmann at the ETH Zurich in 1975 the term "Ticino School" was coined by Kenneth Frampton in 1978. And the aim has been achieved: interpretations that were formulated far away from the epicenter of the building work have created a must-see architecture for architecture afficionados and a veritable export hit. Architects such as Mario Botta,

Während zahlreicher Aufenthalte im Haus in den letzten zehn Jahren ist es nicht selten vorgekommen, dass Einzelpersonen, kleinere Bürogruppen |Fig. 81/82| oder grössere Studierendengruppen vor der Casa Kalman standen. Manchmal angekündigt, meistens aber unangekündigt. War die Besitzerin im Haus, war es möglich, den Bau zu besichtigen. Sie schätzt die Casa Kalman ungemein, ist von ihren Qualitäten überzeugt und möchte andere daran teilhaben lassen. Das Engagement der Besitzerinnen und Besitzer spielt eine massgebliche Rolle innerhalb der Baukultur.

Neben dieser Haltung der Bauherrin wurde dem Haus auch eine andere Art von Wertschätzung entgegengebracht. An das Grundstück schliesst westlich ein nicht minder steiles Areal an, das ebenfalls als Bauland gewidmet ist. Wie bereits erwähnt, wurde dieses Grundstück im Sommer 1996 von Vera Brunner-Kalman gemeinsam mit ihren beiden Kindern angekauft. Damit sollte gewährleistet werden, dass der Blick vom Haus und von der Terrasse auch in Zukunft in der Weise erhalten bleibt, wie es von den Architekten geplant und ausgeführt wurde. Das im Osten befindliche grosse Landstück konnte nicht erstanden werden, aber es wurde 2019 die östlich des Riale Ramnosa gelegene Garage angekauft. Auch hier stand im Vordergrund, die Sicht auf das ikonische Gebäude nicht durch bauliche Veränderungen in nächster Nähe einzuschränken.

Fig. 82

Besichtigung des Büros Trinkler Stula Achille Architekten, Basel, 2021 /
Visit of the architecture office Trinkler Stula Achille Architekten, Basel, 2021

Tita Carloni, Aurelio Galfetti, Livio Vacchini and Flora Ruchat-Roncati, as well as several others, erected numerous buildings in Ticino, and many of these planners also obtained national and international commissions. The buildings of Ticino are included in the travel plans of people who make architecture, culture or study trips and Luigi Snozzi's buildings are fixed stops on such itineraries.

Alongside the themes and outline conditions described above, which define the culture of building during a certain period, further aspects are mentioned here that could be useful in achieving a better understanding of architecture.

Until just a few years ago a key to Casa Kalman was kept in Snozzi's office. Whenever a request was made for a tour of the house, it was generally possible to view it, either with Luigi Snozzi himself or with one of his staff—naturally only after consultation with the owner. As it was and still is so well-known, there is considerable incentive to make a visit and up to the present-day hundreds of people with an interest in architecture have availed of the opportunity to experience the building in reality.

On many visits to the house in the past ten years it was not unusual to find individuals, smaller office groups | Figs. 81/82 |, or larger groups of students standing in front of the Casa Kalman. Some of them had given advance notice of their visit, most had not. If the owner was at home, it was generally possible to visit the building. She values the Casa Kalman enormously, is convinced of its qualities and wants to let others share them. In the culture of building the commitment of owners plays a key role.

In addition to the client's positive attitude, this house also received another, somewhat different kind of appreciation. To the west of the site there is another, equally steep plot, which is also zoned as building land. As already mentioned, this site was acquired by Vera Brunner-Kalman and her two children in summer 1996. The aim was to ensure that the view from the house and from the terrace will be preserved for the future the way it was planned and formed by the architect. It was not possible to acquire the large plot to the east, but in 2019 the garage to the east of the Riale Ramnosa was bought. Here, too, the principal goal was to prevent the view of the iconic house being impaired by any changes that might be made to nearby buildings.

Epilog

Die Casa Kalman steht wie ein künstlicher Fels in einem Meer aus amorphem Siedlungsbrei und verkündet wie eh und je verheissungsvoll die architektonischen, städtebaulichen und ästhetischen Prinzipien ihres Autors und ihrer Zeit. Nicht nur die Bekanntheit des Gebäudes lässt einen aufblicken, passiert man die Casa Kalman. Das Verhältnis von Natur und menschlichem Eingriff, die künstlerische Formfindung und gleichzeitig die kontextuelle Arbeit, das Reagieren auf die Topografie und die Berücksichtigung der Orientierung machen das Bauwerk zu einem Markstein der Architektur der 1970er-Jahre.

Dieses Artefakt, aus dem modernen Baustoff Beton, ist in der Praxis der Tessiner Architektur der Nachkriegszeit verortet. |Fig. 83| Der vom Menschen geschaffene Kunststein ist im südlichsten Schweizer Kanton omnipräsent und wird für infrastrukturelle Bauten ebenso wie für Büro-, Geschäfts- und Wohnbauten verwendet. Der im Tessin spät einsetzende Wirtschaftsaufschwung und der Bauboom fielen zusammen mit der Erfolgsgeschichte des kostengünstig herzustellenden, einfach anzuwendenden und leicht formbaren Materials. |Fig. 84| Stolz steht die Casa Kalman da, in Würde gealtert,

Fig. 83   Detail des Balkons / Detail of the balcony

Epilogue

The Casa Kalman stands like an artificial rock in a sea of amorphous settlements and proclaims, as auspiciously as ever, the architectural, urban design and aesthetic principles of its author and its time. It is not just the fact that the building is so well-known that causes you to look upwards as you pass the Casa Kalman. The relationship between nature and human intervention, the artistic discovery of form and, at the same time, the contextual work, the response to the topography and the reflections about the orientation all combine to make this building a milestone in the architecture of the 1970s.

This artefact, built of concrete, the modern construction material, is rooted in the practice of Ticino architecture of the post-war era. |Fig. 83| This artificial "stone" is ubiquitous in Switzerland's southernmost canton, where it is used for infrastructure buildings as well as for office blocks, commercial and residential buildings. The economic and construction boom, which came relatively late to Ticino, coincided with the success story of this economically produced, simply used, and easily formed material. |Fig. 84| The Casa Kalman stands proudly, aging with dignity in as far as, given the minimal patina of concrete, which is practically indestructible, one can speak here of aging at all. The incision made by house and terrace in the landscape appears martial, massive, and final. |Fig. 85/86| Today—at a time overshadowed by the climate crisis and discourses about the sustainable use of resources and the recyclability of building elements—one reads the Casa Kalmann as the work of a bygone era. But this in no way diminishes the fascination exerted by Snozzi's work. On the contrary, some of the lessons that can be learned from it may be of decisive importance for thinking and building in the future.

Overshadowed by the dominant, permanently effective, formal, and material presence of the house, the vegetation in the surroundings has changed continuously. It is subject to constant change. The planting played a significant role in Snozzi's overall conception, as a planting plan produced in the office shows. A few trees and shrubs from the time the house was built (fig, sycamore, hazelnut) have survived to the present day. Other plants grew from seeds blown by the wind (walnut) or were planted by the present owner. The architect even envisaged that parts of the house would be overgrown by Virginia creeper. For many years this was the case in the northern area of the house, as is shown by pictures in Internet. |Fig. 87| A few years ago the owner

Epilog

Fig. 84   Nordfassade / Northern façade

sofern man bei der minimen Patina auf dem schier unverwüstlichen Beton überhaupt von altern sprechen kann. Der Einschnitt von Haus und Terrasse in der Landschaft scheint martialisch, massiv und endgültig.
Fig. 85/86 Heute – in einer Zeit, die überschattet ist von einer Klimakrise und von Diskursen über die nachhaltige Ressourcenverwendung und die Wiederverwendbarkeit von Bauteilen – liest man die Casa Kalman als ein Werk einer vergangenen Epoche. Doch das tut der Faszination, die dieses Werk Snozzis ausstrahlt, keinen Abbruch. Im Gegenteil, so manche Lehre, die daraus zu ziehen ist, kann für ein Denken und Bauen der Zukunft von entscheidender Wichtigkeit sein.

    Im Schatten der dominanten, dauerhaft wirkenden, formalen und materiellen Präsenz des Hauses hat sich die vegetative Umgebung kontinuierlich verändert. Sie ist einem steten Wandel unterworfen. Die Bepflanzung spielte schon für Snozzis Gesamtkonzeption eine wesentliche Rolle, wie dies ein Grünplan aus dem Büro beweist. Wenige Bäume und Sträucher aus der Entstehungszeit (Feigenbaum, Bergahorn, Haselstrauch) haben sich bis heute erhalten. Andere Pflanzen entstanden aus wild ausgesätem Samen (Walnussbaum)

Epilogue

Fig. 85 — Westfassade / Western façade

Fig. 86 — Austritt bei der Küche / Small terrace near the kitchen

Fig. 87 Schrägansicht von Südost, 2003 / Oblique view from southeast, 2003

Fig. 88 Pflanzenreste auf der Nordfassade / Plan residues on the north façade

Epilogue

Fig. 89 — Pflanzenreste auf dem Beton / Plant residues on the concrete

had this planting removed. Dried-out suckers and tendrils on the north wall still indicate the former vegetation as a temporal layer. |Figs. 88/89|

In much the same way as plants form the organic setting for the house, the fauna—birds, squirrels, and insects—bring life to the house and its surroundings. |Figs. 90/91| If you are in the house, walk through the rooms, open the windows and doors to ventilate the space, or walk out onto the terrace, each time you see a small spectacle of nature. After having taken just a few steps along the terrace, any time between April and November you encounter a stream of ants busily crossing from one side to the other. Nature, too, has subjugated the house, has incorporated it into its world, and has accepted it.

Fig. 90 — Licht und Schatten im Schlafzimmergeschoss / Light and shadow on the bedroom floor

oder wurden durch die jetzige Besitzerin gepflanzt. Der Architekt sah sogar vor, dass das Haus durch wilden Wein in Teilen überwuchert werde. Über Jahre hinweg war dies im nördlichen Bereich des Hauses auch der Fall, wie dies auf Bildern im World Wide Web zu sehen ist. |Fig. 87| Vor wenigen Jahren liess die Besitzerin schliesslich diesen Bewuchs entfernen. An der Nordwand bilden die eingetrockneten Saugnäpfe und Ranken die ehemalige Begrünung als Zeitschicht noch ab. |Fig. 88/89|

Genauso wie die Pflanzen die organische Umgebung des Hauses bilden, verhält es sich auch mit der Fauna. |Fig. 90/91| Vögel, Eichhörnchen und Insekten beleben das Haus und dessen Umgebung. Ist man im Haus und geht durch die Räume, öffnet die Fenster und Türen zum Durchlüften oder betritt die Terrasse, so wird einem jedes Mal ein kleines Naturspektakel gewahr. Nach wenigen Schritten begegnet man von April bis November einem emsigen Ameisenstrom, der die Terrasse quert, um von der einen Seite zur anderen zu gelangen. Auch die Natur hat sich das Haus untertan gemacht, es einverleibt in ihre Welt und es angenommen.

Fig. 91 Bergahorn und Südfassade / Sycamore maple and southern façade

Dank

Für die Realisierung dieses Buchvorhabens ist an erster Stelle Annette Helle (Institutsleitung) sowie Oswald Hari (Studiengangleitung Bachelor) vom Institut Architektur an der FHNW Muttenz zu danken. Für ihre Grosszügigkeit und Offenheit bin ich Vera Brunner-Kalman zu ausserordentlichem Dank verpflichtet. Den beiden Fotografen, Giaime Meloni und Julian Salinas, die das Haus mit ihren Fotoapparaten eingefangen haben, gebührt grosser Respekt und ebenso grosser Dank. Darüber hinaus haben dankenswerterweise Leandro Villalba, Vera Brunner-Kalman, Elke Ehret sowie Hans-Jürgen Breuning Fotografien zur Verfügung gestellt. Die Mitarbeiterin des Archivio del Moderno, Micaela Caletti-Zonca, hat mit omnipräsenter Hilfsbereitschaft meine Recherchen erleichtert und die Bildbeschaffung speditiv erledigt. Dem Vizedirektor des Archivs, Dr. Nicola Navone, sei für seine grosszügige Unterstützung ebenso herzlich gedankt. Bei Torsten Korte möchte ich mich herzlich für seine Hilfestellung bei der Kontaktaufnahme mit dem Archiv sowie bei heiklen Übersetzungsfragen danken.

Die konzeptionelle und gestalterische Umsetzung der Inhalte in ein ansprechendes Buch besorgten Pascal Storz und Fabian Bremer mit Unterstützung von Hannes Drißner. Die Umschlagillustration wurde von ihnen gemeinsam mit Moritz Wick entwickelt, und Henning Weiss hat drei Pläne gezeichnet. Ihnen ist für ihre ästhetisch ansprechende grafische Gestaltung und zeichnerische Arbeit herzlichst zu danken. Ebenso sei Roderick O'Donovan für seine ausserordentlich gelungene Übersetzung sowie Silke Rabus und Doris Tranter für ihr präzises Lektorat und Korrektorat gedankt.

Dem Leiter des Christoph Merian Verlags, Oliver Bolanz, sowie der dortigen Lektorats- und Herstellungsverantwortlichen Iris Becher und den beiden Mitarbeiterinnen im Marketing, Andrea Bikle und Karin Matt, danke ich für die unkomplizierte und stets freundliche und wohlwollende Hilfestellung.

Wenn dieses Buch den geschätzten Leserinnen und Lesern Freude bereitet, sie Interesse an dem Inhalt finden und auf diese Weise Einblicke in die Baukultur des Tessins und der Schweiz erhalten haben, hat sich der Aufwand mehr als gelohnt.

Acknowledgements

For the realization of this book project, I would like to thank first and foremost Annette Helle (head of the institute) and Oswald Hari (head of the Bachelor's program) from the Institute of Architecture at the FHNW Muttenz. For her generosity and openness, I am extraordinarily indebted to Vera Brunner-Kalman. The two photographers, Giaime Meloni and Julian Salinas, who captured the house with their cameras, deserve great respect and equally great thanks. In addition, Leandro Villalba, Vera Brunner-Kalman, Elke Ehret as well as Hans-Jürgen Breuning have kindly provided photographs. The staff member of the Archivio del Moderno, Micaela Caletti-Zonca, facilitated my research with omnipresent helpfulness and handled the acquisition of images expeditiously. I would also like to thank the vice-director of the archive, Dr. Nicola Navone, for his generous support. I would like to sincerely thank Torsten Korte for his assistance in contacting the archive as well as in delicate translation issues.

Pascal Storz and Fabian Bremer with the help of Hannes Drißner were responsible for the conceptual and creative implementation of the contents in an attractive book. The cover illustration was developed by them together with Moritz Wick, and Henning Weiss drew three plans. They deserve my sincere thanks for their aesthetically pleasing graphic design and drawing work. Thanks are also due to Roderick O'Donovan for his exceptionally successful translation as well as to Silke Rabus and Doris Tranter for their precise editing and proofreading.

I would also like to thank the head of Christoph Merian Verlag, Oliver Bolanz, as well as Iris Becher, the editor and production manager there, and the two marketing staff members, Andrea Bikle and Karin Matt, for their uncomplicated and always friendly and benevolent assistance.

If this book gives pleasure to the esteemed readers, if they develop an interest in the contents and in this way discover insights into the architecture of Ticino and Switzerland, then the effort involved will have proved more than worthwhile.

Datenblatt / Data Sheet

Adresse / Address:	Via Panoramica 66, 6645 Brione sopra Minusio, Tessin / Ticino (Das Grundstück liegt jedoch auf dem Gemeindegebiet von Minusio / the site, however, is in the municipal district of Minusio)
Grundstücksgrösse / Site area:	756 m²
Planer / Planners:	Luigi Snozzi Walter von Euw
Geometer / Surveyor:	Ing. Ivo Buetti
Bauingenieur / Civil engineer:	Ing. P. Bondietti
Vorgaben der Kommune / Requirements of the municipality:	14. September 1973 / September 14, 1973 Die Ausnutzungsziffer von 0.15 erlaubt bei einer Grundstücksfläche von 756 m² eine Geschossfläche von 113,40 m² / For a site area of 756 m² the floor area ratio of 0.15 allowed a total floor area of 113.40 m² Höhe: 7,5 m / Height: 7.5 m Zwei Wohngeschosse / Two residential stories Abstand von Grundstücksgrenze: 4,0 m / Distance from site boundary: 4.0 m
Planungs- und Bauzeit / Planning and construction period:	Mitte / mid 1973 – Mitte / mid 1976
Kosten / Costs:	Grundstück / Site 60.000 CHF Baukosten / Construction costs 268.672 CHF Architektenhonorar / Architect's fee 29.000 CHF

Quellen / Sources

Monografien / Monographs

Croset, Pierre-Alain (Red.): *Luigi Snozzi. progetti e architetture. 1957–1984.* Milano: Electa 1984.

Disch, Peter: *Luigi Snozzi, Costruire e progetti – Buildings and projects 1958–1993.* Lugano: ADV Publishing House 1994.

Lichtenstein, Claude: *Luigi Snozzi.* Basel / Boston / Berlin: Birkhäuser 1997.

Museum für Gestaltung (Hg. / Ed.) / Steiger, Bruno (Red.): *Luigi Snozzi. Auf den Spuren des Ortes.* Schriftenreihe / Museum für Gestaltung Zürich 21. Zürich: Eigenverlag von Schule und Museum für Gestaltung 1996.

Rimmel, Maximilian / Edition Bibliothek Werner Oechslin (Hg. / Ed.): *Luigi Snozzi. 25 Aphorismen zur Architektur.* Basel: Schwabe Verlag 2013.

Werner, Frank / Schneider, Sabine: *Neue Tessiner Architektur.* Stuttgart: Deutsche Verlags-Anstalt 1989.

Zeitschriften / Magazines

a+u. A Monthly Journal of World Architecture and Urbanism. Nr. / No. 69, Tokyo 1976.

Architecture aujourdhui. Nr. / No. 236, Paris 1984.

archithese. Zeitschrift und Schriftenreihe für Architektur und Kunst. Heft / issue 3–84, Jg. / vol. 14, Zürich 1984.

du. Nr. / No. 11, Zürich 1989.

rivista tecnica della Svizzera italiana. Nr. / No. 12, Lugano 1977.

werk archithese. Zeitschrift und Schriftenreihe für Architektur und Kunst. Heft / issue 9, Jg. / vol. 64, Zürich 1977.

World Wide Web

https://journals.openedition.org/craup/4263?lang=en

https://ofhouses.com/post/640623352484102144/863-luigi-snozzi-kalmann-house-minusio

https://www.architectenwerk.nl/architectuur/A-visites/01.htm

https://www.northernarchitecture.us/housing-project/bankinter-79.html

https://www.sosbrutalism.org/cms/18891619

https://www.thomasdeckker.co.uk/publications/issues_4.htm

https://www.youtube.com/watch?v=la-l0yXt9-Q

https://www.youtube.com/watch?v=YSJ37FCZ9Hs&t=375s

Impressum / Colophon

Herausgeber / Editor
swissmonographies:
Harald R. Stühlinger

Lektorat / Editorial reading:
Silke Rabus, Wien;
Doris Tranter, Basel

Übersetzung / Translation:
Roderick O'Donovan, Wien

Konzept und Gestaltung /
Design concept:
Pascal Storz, Berlin;
Fabian Bremer, Leipzig;
mit / with Hannes Drißner,
Leipzig

Umschlagabbildung /
Cover illustration:
Moritz Wick, Zürich

Satz / Typesetting:
Hannes Drißner, Leipzig

Bildbearbeitung /
Lithography:
DZA Druckerei zu
Altenburg GmbH,
Altenburg

Druck und Bindung /
Printing and binding:
DZA Druckerei
zu Altenburg GmbH,
Altenburg

Schrift / Typeface:
Union

Papier / Paper:
Munken Print White 15,
MaxiGloss,
Profitop opak

Bibliografische Information der Deutschen Nationalbibliothek: Die Deutsche Nationalbibliothek verzeichnet diese Publikation in der Deutschen Nationalbibliografie; detaillierte bibliografische Daten sind im Internet über http://dnb.dnb.de abrufbar.

Bibliographic information published by the Deutsche Nationalbibliothek: The Deutsche Nationalbibliothek lists this publication in the Deutsche Nationalbibliografie; detailed bibliographic data is available on the Internet at http://dnb.dnb.de.

Unveränderter Nachdruck 2023
© 2022 Christoph Merian Verlag

© 2022 Texte / Texts:
Harald R. Stühlinger

© 2022 Abbildungen /
Illustrations:
siehe Bildnachweis /
see Photo credits

Alle Rechte vorbehalten; kein Teil dieses Werkes darf in irgendeiner Form ohne vorherige schriftliche Genehmigung des Verlags reproduziert oder unter Verwendung elektronischer Systeme verarbeitet, vervielfältigt oder verbreitet werden.

All rights reserved; no part of this publication may be reproduced, stored in a retrieval system or transmitted in any form or by any means, electronic, mechanical, photocopying, recording or otherwise, without prior written permission from the publisher.

ISBN 978-3-85616-978-7

www.merianverlag.ch

Bildnachweis /
Photo credits

Leandro Villalba:
Einstiegsbildstrecke /
Opening image spreads,
Fig. 57, 61

Henning Weiss:
Fig. 1, 3, 11

Julian Salinas:
Fig. 2, 6–8, 10, 17, 21–22, 25, 29–30, 56, 65–67, 73, 75–76, 84, 89–90

Giaime Meloni:
Fig. 4, 5, 9, 12–16, 18–20, 23–24, 26–28, 31, 59–60, 63–64, 74, 77–80, 83, 85–86, 88, 91, Abschlussbildstrecke / Closing image spreads, Umschlagbild Rückseite / Back cover

Archivio del Moderno, Balerna, Nachlass /
Estate of Luigi Snozzi:
Fig. 32–55, 71–72

Vera Brunner-Kalman:
Fig. 58, 62

Bibliothek FHNW:
Fig. 68–70

Elke Ehret:
Fig. 81–82

Hans-Jürgen Breuning:
Fig. 87

Verein zur
Erforschung der
europäischen Stadt

n|w Fachhochschule Nordwestschweiz
Hochschule für Architektur, Bau und Geomatik